About t

Annie Cardone spent many years travelling the world as a model before finally settling down and building a career as a marketing executive in England and the United States of America.

Over the past twenty-five years Annie has worked as a volunteer in her spare time. Teaching communication skills to women who have suffered childhood trauma, violence and abuse, so they can learn how to navigate life and take better care of themselves by setting boundaries is something she is passionate about.

Menopause is different for everyone. Going through the change herself, Annie found that so many women did not have access to doctors, endocrinologists and important information and therefore had limited understanding on how menopause affects not just the body but also the mind. Women have no idea that menopause can be the most dangerous time of life psychologically if you are not armed with information on how to take care of yourself.

As a human rights activist and humanitarian Annie spends her time researching this topic to help others. If she is not typing one hundred words a minute for her latest project then you can find Annie on her road bike, training for charity rides across England, Ireland, France and America.

MENOPAUSE WTH!

ANNIE CARDONE

MENOPAUSE WTH!

Vanguard Press

A CIP catalogue record for this title is
available from the British Library.

ISBN 978 1 80016 217 4

*Vanguard Press is an imprint of
Pegasus Elliot MacKenzie Publishers Ltd.*
www.pegasuspublishers.com

First Published in 2022

**Vanguard Press
Sheraton House Castle Park
Cambridge England**

Printed & Bound in Great Britain

Dedication

Dedicated to my sister Kay O'Connor for
always believing in me.

Acknowledgements

It is 'thank you' time and I feel a sense of achievement. Years of journaling about my menopause journey, for seven years, all came together, and I wrote a book!

First of all, I could not have put this book together without the help and support of my family. They stood by me through it all. My mother's unconditional love was paramount as we battled to find out what was wrong with me. Her medical knowledge of the endocrine system was invaluable; I would not have made it without her.

To my sister Kay who I miss every day. She came to my side and helped me see the light. She showed me where I was going wrong with my hormone health, by allowing myself to take on the stress of so many toxic people. Thank God, she made it so very clear that enough was enough. I will never live up to her; she was truly an angel and a total one of a kind. Forever missed but always with me.

Thank you to my Church who always had a candle lit in the dark moments where there was no light in my life. Thankfully they understood what I was going through. One particular friend who wrote about the endocrine system years ago, helped me enormously. He understood it in a way no one else could. He paved the way for me to survive through his writings and teachings. He taught me the endocrine system is the communication channel from the mind to the body. The delicate balance of hormones can be altered by the slightest thing such as stress and suppression, so attention must be paid to its care and causes of upset in order to have control over it. He understood the mechanisms of the mind so well and taught me that earlier incidents in your life, containing pain and loss, can be repeated over and over when they are triggered by a similar setup in the present day. So each time a woman experiences a menopause storm she goes through the same physical problems each and every time.

Each time my mind and body crashed during menopause it was almost identical to the first time. The same physical symptoms, insomnia and sleep psychosis played out again and again. The only thing that helped me was knowing exactly what was happening and how to bring myself out of a tail spin. I was taught by him that my mental health was directly impacted by my physical health. In fact I discovered over time that even something as simple as a chest infection or a bladder infection, which is extremely common in menopausal women, can impact your hormones so drastically that your mental health rapidly deteriorates at the same time as your body and left without treatment or antibiotics can be fatal as you become extremely ill.

All this knowledge armed me with the tools I needed to fight off psychiatric evaluations and recommendations for medication that would have made my life and health worse.

Without coming across this vital education and understanding I would probably be a brain-dead vegetable through electroshock treatment by now. That is not being dramatic; that is just the basic truth of the situation due to the fact that the relationship between mental health, mental disorders and menopause is not well understood.

Finally, to all the women out there who have come across this book. I hope you find some comfort in knowing we are all in this together. I will continue to write, research and campaign for better treatment for those who suffer.

One day we will make the world a safer place to experience hormone fluctuations. We've had them our whole lives; as teenagers, through pregnancy, through IVF, through post-natal depression, perimenopause, menopause and even post-menopause. We need to finally put an end to the barbaric treatment women receive at the hands of psychiatrists due to menopause. These women just wanted help with their symptoms and all they got was incorrect data and spiritual abuse through the over-prescribing of highly addictive antidepressants and sleep medications, dished out to alarming degree by doctors who have targets to hit for the pharmaceutical companies. It is truly unbelievable how many women have either committed suicide on these drugs or died from being prescribed lithium for the menopause.

It is the women who are not financially well off that are the real target. Good healthcare is expensive and even within the NHS, educated doctors who understand the endocrine system are few and far between. You cannot even rely on your general practitioner to know much about your hormones; most of them are completely lost on this subject and freely admit it. More education and awareness is needed so that we can take care of ourselves and recognize the signs and triggers that are endocrine created but impact our emotional and mental health to such a degree that we end up in the wrong hands.

Contents

Foreword

I am a survivor of a toxic, abusive and dysfunctional childhood and sadly this is not unusual. The experience left me suffering from post-traumatic stress disorder, crippling insecurity and self-doubt. On the downside, I had been dealt a bad hand, but on the upside, my childhood gave me an inner strength and will to survive that is undeniable to anyone who knows me. Navigating life with this as my foundation was not an easy task, and many times I had to learn the hard way as I had no role models when it came to relationships and family life. Terrified of love and abandonment, I kept on the move and never stayed anywhere too long.

This poor start in life had a huge impact on everything and when I arrived in my mid-forties and perimenopause hit, I hit a wall that stopped me in my tracks and gave me no choice but to stop running and start making peace with the past. Menopause and mental health were a battle I did not see coming so it was shocking that it destroyed my life in so many ways.

Growing up I was curious about everything. This fierce questioning mind of mine just would not quit, which turned out to be my saving grace years later as I tried to work out the complicated tricks my endocrine system started playing on my mind during menopause. Through the complicated transition I tried to find the answers as to what was wrong with me as the menopausal symptoms affected not just my body but also my mind.

During this time as I tried to find out more about my hormones I was cast into a world of confusing medical terms, misinformation and contradictory viewpoints that left me with no answers. I soon started to feel that no one really knew what the hell they were talking about and can only liken the process as trying to finish a jigsaw puzzle when half of the pieces are missing: you will never do it! You have to find the missing pieces. Searching for the missing pieces of information about menopause and its connection and impact on the mind was the most frustrating thing I have ever done, with one step forward and two steps back the whole way through.

On my eight-year journey through menopause hell and back again I was hospitalized four times due to oestrogen dominance, which causes insomnia and sleep psychosis. I now know menopause to be the most underestimated physical and psychological health issue known to womankind that can impact your mental health as a knock-on effect. Unfortunately, not many people know, understand or accept that the side effects can be life threatening. The hardest part in writing this book was remembering what happened during the downward hormonal spiral due to sleep deprivation which caused sleep psychosis. So much of what I went through is a fog and in some situations I had total amnesia as my mind shut down and I was in a sleep state walking around. It was terrifying.

The two biggest contributors to a hormonal roller coaster is stress and amazingly enough being around toxic people. Just one person, close to you, with supposedly your best interests at heart can distract you from taking care of yourself because your focus is on them and their problems rather than your own. These individuals can suck the life literally out of you with a smile on their face and a knife behind their back. These two factors have a major impact on your endocrine system and by understanding the mechanics of how this works you can turn your life and menopause around.

Women have a tendency to put everyone before themselves and when they hit overwhelm and are not able to manage the constant stress that is being brought into their lives, it has a devastating effect on the endocrine system, which creates a chemical imbalance and then you can physically and mentally start down.

As with airline safety procedure, the rule for frontline emergency services is that they must ensure they're safe before helping anyone else, and at this time in our life, going through menopause, it is imperative that women do the same. Women have a habit of making sure everyone else is ok and often neglect their own needs. It makes sense that in order to take care of anyone you have to be in good shape otherwise everything can fall apart. This has never been truer than when you hit menopausal age and you have so many responsibilities, people to look after and mouths to feed.

Finding your balance and practising self-care by setting strict boundaries with others, who are overly dependent on us, is one of the first steps to handle stress. The more stress you have in your life, the more the endocrine struggles to stabilise. It impacts us physically, emotionally, intellectually and spiritually. Many of us have no idea what is happening and do not even make the connection between stress and menopause. We just know we feel like shit most of the time and the constant exhaustion will not quit but we are helpless to stop it.

Many years ago, human beings had a much shorter life span and we only lived until about forty-five years old. Women would have died due to the symptoms of menopause. Today we live much longer lives and have to work out how to cope with the total depletion of vital hormones that keep us alive. These hormones coat the neurons in the brain that are responsible for our short- and long-term cognitive memory, so it is no wonder our mind starts to short circuit. When the hormones deplete the neurons fuse and short circuit and our thinking and ability to manage day to day life crashes.

This is a story of learning how to trust ourselves and know our limitations. Writing this book has been a rite of passage and even though I am not a medical professional I know first-hand what it feels like to be on the menopause train and have had days when I was barely hanging on due to exhaustion. At the end of this journey, I feel like a victorious warrior, who fought and won and never gave up because I had nothing left to lose. My many battles over this time have shown me who I am and what I stand for and so I have written this book to raise awareness and to help other women who have suffered and been failed completely by the healthcare system. I want women to know that we do not have to suffer in silence; our stories need to be told so we can come together and support each other and not feel alone and suffocated by the shame, humiliation and embarrassment of our journey.

We have a voice and a platform now through social media and we can use it. Every one of us can be brave and share our stories with our heads held high. This is the only way we will win.

Of course, to fully understand where my problems began, we have to delve back into the roller coaster I call my past, as it is in our childhoods that we get set up to fail in practising self-care.

1

Menopause: A Unique Journey

Have you ever felt that you are crazy, out of control, over-reactive, impatient, moody, unbalanced, constantly exhausted, stressed out, overwhelmed, anxious, neurotic, lonely and depressed? You are not alone. Welcome to the joys of the endocrine system and your hormones, which can be your best friend and your worst enemy in exactly the same moment. Although so many women experience menopause differently, we all share one thing in common and that is the fact that you cannot avoid it. In some way or another it will impact our lives and the lives of those we love. It is staggering how much data has been written about it yet there is one thing that seems to be touched on least of all and that is the impact it has on your mind, emotions and reactions to everyday life.

If you had told me eight years ago what lay ahead, I would have never believed it. I went from being a happy, hard-working, energetic, fun-loving person to someone who was unrecognisable. It was as if I literally woke up one day and I was different and the world around me had completely changed and not for the better. This book covers some basic facts about menopause that we all assume everyone knows but you would be surprised if you knew that was not the case. Due to the fact that I had such little information about the endocrine system, left me vulnerable to the judgement and viewpoint of others. I obviously knew menopause affected a woman physically, but I was seriously looking forward to my menstrual cycle disappearing and was going to welcome a few hot flashes as a trade-off. No one told me or warned me of the impact it would have on my mind. Life was never going to be the same again and I just did not see it coming.

There are over six thousand women per day entering menopause in the United States alone. With numbers as staggering as this, you would think we would have a better understanding and more awareness as to the endocrine system. Menopausal symptoms are very different from person to person. For some it is a very simple process, a few hot sweats and that is it. I know women who breeze through it, and I have now met many who, like me, do not. For some, hormone replacement therapy will handle the irritating symptoms such as hot flashes, night sweats, headaches and the mind fog that is so debilitating you just want to stay in bed for a month. We are not all the same as our brain chemicals and endocrine systems are unique to us individually.

I am not a medical expert but after my experience going through perimenopause and menopause, I know more than I did and enough to have kept me alive. This book is an account of my story from beginning to the present time, laying out all the contributing factors that led me down the path of hormone hell and what steps I took to get back in control of my life. By facing the truth about the external factors that impeded my recovery, such as stress and toxic people, I realised how much these two factors played a part in whether I got better or worse. Eventually I had to change the way I was living, loving and doing life if I was to live to see my old age. Thankfully, I now have a tried and tested formula and routine that I want to share with you so you can do the same.

Before we go into this in more depth here are some menopause terms and definitions that lay a foundation for understanding what we are dealing with.

Perimenopause: it is the time when the ovaries gradually produce less oestrogen. It commonly happens a year or so prior to menopause.

Menopause: the ceasing of menstruation. This is the time when you no longer have your periods, and you are now officially in menopause.

Hysteria: uterus (suffering in that area). Women are sometimes given hysterectomies to help suffering with their reproductive organs. This would catapult them into menopause.

So, let's now explore how stress plays a part in your menopause symptoms. Here is a list which covers the more popular ones, but I am sure there are many more:

Hot flushes
Night sweats

Difficulty sleeping
Vaginal dryness
Reduced libido
Headaches
Mood swings
Sadness
Anxiety
Heart palpitations
Urinary Tract Infections (UTIs)
Weak bones (osteoporosis)

These are just the common physical symptoms that mostly we have heard of. What this book is going to address is the ones that are not spoken about so openly and freely, and that is how menopause affects your mental health, the mind and your well-being emotionally and reactively.

The first thing to understand is that your hormone levels are constantly changing on a daily or hourly basis depending on what is going on in your life and how much stress you are under. To find a place of stability can be fleeting, especially if your life is already a struggle, which it can be for many women at this time of life. This is when we start to have health issues, relationship break-ups, hormonal teenagers in the house, financial stress, loss of loved ones, heavy workloads and the list goes on.

Life is not static, meaning it does not stay the same for long periods of time and therefore as life changes and challenges us, it makes sense that chemically we change with it. To find a balanced state and homeostasis is almost impossible but add to this a dysfunctional childhood that did not equip us to cope with life and we really can be in trouble because during troubled childhoods we may not have the basics of self-care. In fact, I believe self-care should be something children learn in school as part of the curriculum. Many children who grow up in a war zone tend to be trained to look after everyone else but themselves.

There is no doubt in my mind that unhandled stress ramps up menopause symptoms and the problem is that we are controlled by events outside ourselves that contribute to our own emotions and stress. There is no way to avoid the bad things that happen in life and the stressful impact these events have on us individually, however, there is a way to minimise the damage and set our lives up for balance on a regular basis no matter what is thrown at us. So, the question is why does stress create havoc with our hormones? Here is a quick biology lesson on the impact of stress on your mind and body.

The endocrine system is very complex and not very well understood but one thing that I found to be true was that chronic stress leads to elevated or depleted hormones such as progesterone and oestrogen especially during menopause. Cortisol is one of the most important hormones that is not discussed as much as all the others and it is actually one of the most important ones as it is the stress hormone and can be a huge factor in menopausal symptoms. Cortisol and Serotonin are important because they regulate biological processes such as sleep, appetite, energy, and sex drive. They allow the emotional range of normal moods to be expressed and without these hormones we are totally at the mercy of the environment which impacts us and impinges on us the daily onslaught of stress. This creates a roller coaster as when our hormones go out of whack we do not have full control of our emotions and one minute can be so happy and the next in despair which is all connected to the balance our hormones have from one minute to the next.

There are some life circumstances that are totally unavoidable, for example the death of a loved one. The body's response is one of overwhelming grief and emotion causing stress on the system. The hypothalamus is located in your brain and works as the traffic lights to release and retract your adrenal glands from flooding the body with a hormone called cortisol. When we suffer a devastating loss, it triggers high levels of cortisol to be released into the body which is extremely toxic and is manifested physically in the following ways: fatigue, anxiety, insomnia, intestinal inflammation, weight gain, type II diabetes, immune disorders such as cancer, depression and hormone imbalances.

This in itself is a long and scary list of things that happen to our body when we are stressed! It is the core issue we all struggle with in life and the only way to get a healthier balance in life is to handle this issue first and foremost. That sounds pretty easy, right?

Well, if handling stress were that easy, we would all have done it by now. For many, a day at the spa with a facial and a massage will melt stress away, and you can feel renewed but unless life changes occur, the day at the spa will be undone the minute you go home and are confronted with the chaos of life. Handling stress seems theoretically pretty simple and obvious but yet we still allow stress to dominate our lives. So how do we start the process of undoing this automatic stress response that happens in our bodies and makes us ill, especially during menopause?

The basic biology of the situation, without getting into big confusing medical terms, is this. Your hormones play a key role in your mental and physical health. They function as the receptors and communicators between the mind and the body through various functions of the brain. On top of this the uterus and the health of the ovaries is directly linked to brain health. Oestrogen is not just a hormone required for reproductive purposes, but it is also responsible for pushing neurons to burn glucose for brain energy. With this in mind you would think that more experts are putting these things together and realising you cannot treat the mind, brain, emotions, body and the endocrine system as separate entities; they have to be looked at and understood as they function with each other, otherwise you are just putting a Band-Aid on one problem without having solved the bigger picture.

On top of this, anatomically there is a part of the brain called the brainstem and its function is to regulate sleep. During menopause when oestrogen is depleted, the brainstem cannot function properly, and sleep issues start occurring. Another part of the brain is called the amygdala and its function is the emotion sensor, meaning that it can control your emotions, and when oestrogen is depleted, it starts to malfunction, creating brain fog, forgetfulness and mood swings.

So, you are not crazy; your brain is just not getting the good nutrition it needs to function well, which is no different from expecting a car to run without putting fuel in it. With both these parts of the brain short-circuiting during menopause or after childbirth, it can start to feel as though your mind is playing tricks on you and it is. There is a reason sleep deprivation was a form of torture during war time as it is extremely effective in driving someone insane.

So, what happens to women who have just been through childbirth, or IVF or who are having hormone fluctuations during menopause, and they start to experience trouble sleeping over a prolonged period of time? Would they be expected to be rational, logical, sane and stable? No, they would not, in fact they would become very ill and start exhibiting psychosis and this is where the trouble really starts, and this is what happened to me. After being hospitalised for sleep psychosis I completely understand the absolute hell it is, for a woman to go through. The sad truth is that when women are admitted to the emergency room in the throes of insomnia, she will be treated as a mental patient intake and diagnosed based on psychosis alone. No consideration will be given to her age and the possibility that this could be a hormone issue so one of the triggers for the psychosis is completely overlooked and ignored at this point. The danger for women in this situation is that they will then be heavily sedated and subjected to a psychiatric evaluation and sent to a psychiatric ward regardless of if they have a mental illness or not

This happens to over 1.5 million women every year in America alone after being admitted to an emergency room for menopausal symptoms such as insomnia. Imagine the numbers if we were to calculate them worldwide. Not one of these women get a hormone test. So many of the doctors in charge of their care have little understanding or knowledge of the endocrine system and no one is taking responsibility for this blatant abuse of vulnerable women.

To prevent this from happening, women have to know the connection between the endocrine system and the mind and be armed and educated so that this cannot continue to happen during menopause or after giving birth. Women worry they are losing their minds when they are going through a hormonal transition that none of us can avoid. With education on this subject, we can not only protect ourselves but also protect future generations.

Looking back when this happened to me in England, I was forty-eight years old and not one single medical expert had an inkling this could be perimenopause or menopause related. My General Practitioner, along with so many doctors today do not have the knowledge or training on the endocrine system to help us. Their "go to" solution is sedation and psychiatric drugs. In fact, doctors now can opt in or out of the menopause segments of their training, it is optional which is very concerning for the millions of women who will go through the same thing as I did. It was only when I went to the USA and a kind doctor called Dr Megan Shields put the pieces together and got me the help I needed. Unfortunately, this amazing woman has since died and along with her went so much knowledge, understanding, kindness and humanity.

Basically, if we do not take care of ourselves during stressful times such as grief, loss and change then our menopausal symptoms will worsen and we could end up in the hands of the wrong people, psychiatrists who have no cure and no solution for menopause. Self-care during menopause is therefore paramount to rest the cortisol clock and turn the cortisol tap off so our bodies can recover and balance out otherwise we risk being labelled insane like women so many years ago who ended up burned as witches at the time of the change. The trouble is that menopause and crashing hormones can make you act and feel insane periodically, so it becomes easy to buy into the solutions presented to us by psychiatry especially when we have nothing else to base our problems on.

We cannot avoid life's trials and tribulations. Events that cause chronic stress such as being laid off, death of a loved one, divorce, natural disasters all contribute and change our chemical make-up. In menopause we are even more powerless to have balance during these times as we are usually not sleeping well either and that makes problems even harder to confront let alone solve. It creates the perfect storm.

Loss of my father and of my sister both induced major stress into my life during perimenopause and into menopause. Experiencing this kind of grief in perimenopause during a hormone crash can really be dangerous and turning it around became a full-time job if I was going to get back to full health and wellness.

For me, the first step was to recognize that my life and that constant problems were perpetuating a downward spiral and I needed to stop the trajectory downwards and take drastic action to get it moving upwards in the right direction of survival instead of succumbing.

Without this first stage of awareness nothing can be achieved. Recognizing that you have allowed stress to build up and remain unhandled is the key to unlocking this trap. Finding out the source of it is a whole new ball game as it can come from places and people that are totally unexpected. The only way back to harmony and balance in my mind and body was to take a step back and make some tough decisions about the people in my life and the impact they were having because nine times out of ten, it is toxic people who are creating the suppression and drama rather than anything else.

My journey to find balance was precarious as balance in life is not a passive state that we achieve and can keep in place. It is a moving target that needs to be worked on daily and it takes self-discipline to attain for any long periods of time. My biggest downfall in life was not respecting the times when I had balance and investigating more closely what created it. Tracking and cultivating some of the things that helped bring balance to my life would have been very helpful and so this is what I started to do so that it would no longer be a fleeting state that if I blinked I would miss it and it would be gone and not come back for a very long time with the randomity of life pushing it further and further away from me and my fight or flight response kicking in subconsciously and pushing myself too hard, tipping the see-saw of overwhelm by taking on too much and rushing into rescue situations that were not even my responsibility. How could I have possibly expected to find balance when I was perpetuating the stress by taking on other people's troubles and problems as if they were my own?

Therefore, if balance was the goal, the first thing I had to get comfortable with was change as there was going to be a great deal of that in my future if I wanted a different outcome.

I had to find the stress off switch and all roads pointed back to self-love and care and handling the compulsion to keep taking on more, whilst already overwhelmed was just another hurdle to get over. The only way to even begin to understand my hard wiring and how I had allowed things to become so bad was to go back to the beginning and look over my past, as far back as I could remember and figure out when this lack of self-worth and lack of self-care started because this is what was perpetuating the problems in menopause I was facing today. So, I took that journey back in the hope of having an 'a-ha' moment that would turn things around. It was brutal at times to revisit my childhood and extremely painful but since taking that step I have not had another issue because I now understand fully that I was the one creating the stress in my life and that alone was leading to the heightened dominant menopause symptom of insomnia.

As you journey back with me, I want you to know that I am not a victim, this is not to gain sympathy or attention, my past is being told to help other women understand how we are trained and conditioned as children to put ourselves last on the list and that carries forward with us in life and into menopause. This way of living destroys our relationships, careers, physical and mental health, and emotional stability.

I have no shadow of a doubt that my sister, Kay O'Connor, would still be with us today if she had put her own health and well-being first but sadly that was not meant to be as our childhood was a war zone and a fight for survival, so we never learned how to take time out for ourselves. This book is written in her honour just a short time after her death. I hope this book impacts your life in a positive way, as much as it has impacted and healed mine writing it.

2

A Letter to my Parents

My father was a successful engineer and raised me to think like one. He told me "Numbers never lie", which has proven to be true many times over when reading my blood work and hormone levels during menopause. My mother had the same steely determination and her motto in life was "where there is a will there's a way" and she was right. With parents like this, it is not surprising I had a solution and answer to anything and everything, sometimes to an annoying degree.

I had always been quick-witted, very cheeky and a bit of a smart ass growing up. I used humour and acted the clown to cover the fundamental truth that I was crippled with self-loathing and a lack of self-worth. Growing up, I thought I was ugly and stupid. I literally craved love, every second of every day because I was starved of it after my mother left when I was six years old due to the violence and beatings she was subjected to by my father. If she had not left, I honestly believe he would have killed her, his rage was that intense. I therefore spent my life terrified of letting anyone get close to me, for fear of being abandoned later on when they realised just how useless I was.

I had no idea the way I felt about myself was all in my head. I was a kind, sweet, lovable little girl but I had been programmed to believe that I was nothing and so to me it was true. This is what happens to a child when they are not seen, heard and validated as a human being. They do not develop in a healthy way if they have been through this kind of abuse, and they spend a lifetime feeling different from the 'normal' kids.

Through this trauma I learned very quickly that I could use humour and banter and played the clown to get people to like me. I also learned that if I could out-fox someone intellectually, it would hide my nervousness and fear in social situations. Being visible was very dangerous for me as a child, as my siblings and I were targets for my father's aggression and violence after my mother left. Being seen was never a good thing in my book, so I spent a great deal of time in hiding and keeping out of the way. If I could have found a way to be invisible that would have been a dream come true.

Children who go through trauma, over a long period of time, also communicate differently to most. They rely on radar and telepathy a great deal of the time because speaking could potentially give away a hiding place to a persecutor. As a survivor of abuse, you have innate, highly tuned inner sensors that pick-up signals and emotions so you can often predict what is coming next for yourself and others. When you have to do this on a daily basis to survive a childhood, it becomes second nature.

My siblings and I all had wicked radar with each other and used it to protect each other all the time. I almost feel bad for the kids who have it easy and are spoiled, as they really do not know what they are missing. I had no idea my radar or sixth sense had a name until someone told me I was an empath. I actually had to look the word up in a dictionary to understand it. The definition is: Empath: a person with the paranormal ability to perceive the mental or emotional state of another individual. This was certainly true of what I was experiencing and also true of many women, as we are the bearers of children and need this ability to keep them safe and be able to sense what is coming. The trouble with being an empath is that you absorb others' pain and problems and if you do not have good boundaries, you can get caught up and lost in problems that are not yours. Even worse is when you start to rescue others at the expense of yourself. That lesson was a tough one to learn as I loved helping people but eventually realised it was not a healthy operating basis.

I believe every human being has the ability to communicate non-verbally and predict what is coming, but we have tuned out that power and become totally reliant on verbal communication and modern technology. It was different for me and my siblings as we had always used our radar to survive the war zone we were raised in and I just knew we were supposed to operate at this level, because I had been doing it for as long as I could remember.

I now see myself as lucky in hindsight. All the tools I used to survive as a child I relied on heavily to survive when my endocrine system became impaired, and I have both my parents to thank for instilling in me a fierce determination to survive. Dad, without you I would not have found the strength and unrelenting determination to overcome my health struggle during menopause, let alone write this book. I most certainly would not be here today if you had not taught me how to stand up for myself.

Raising four children on your own, whilst struggling with diabetes and holding down a full-time job as a brilliant engineer, was no easy task and there are days when I have no idea how you coped with the overwhelm. Being a boxer when you were young must have helped as you learned to fight through the pain and carry on, no matter what. In life you were dealt some serious blows, but you kept getting back up determined to succeed and you passed that character trait on to me.

Raised in London during World War II, the military survival lessons your father taught you made you strong. Who knew, in years to come, I would need the same survival skills, to get through menopause. Thank you for not treating me differently to my brothers, because I was a girl. The pretty dresses and cooking lessons at school were all great, but knowing how to hunt, fish, shoot and box, were even more vital to my journey in life and far more fun. You taught me to think like an engineer, problem solve like a mathematician and hit like a champ. I think my right hook was highly developed by the time I was three years old and has stood me in good stead in life and as a metaphor. I still hear you say to me, "Annie, hit the biggest one first and you won't have trouble with the rest".

We all know families are not perfect and ours was dysfunction at its best, for many different reasons. At times you were the best of dads and then suddenly the worst of dads. You did your best, with what you had available to you, in the form of help, education and understanding. Years later in 2000 we all went to Phoenix, Arizona for family therapy and the end result was worth it. We healed our painful wounds, forgave ourselves and each other for transgressions and asked God's forgiveness for them too. We left the past firmly in the desert and as the sun went down, our bad memories went with them, one last time.

We had found peace at last and no longer needed to be at war with ourselves and the world. I was so grateful we spent the next twelve years fly fishing and being best friends. Travelling with you was always a blast and if we caught some fish along the way, it was a bonus. No one made me laugh more than you. We shared the same silly sense of humour that only we find funny. We also shared a will to survive and a resilience that is second to none.

No matter how hard the psychiatrists hit you with lithium at nineteen years old for diabetes and twelve rounds of electroshock treatment in your fifties, you fought back and still worked out a way to survive without their drugs, even though your short-term memory was shot to pieces. Thankfully, you could still recount all of Mohammed Ali's boxing matches. I watched every one of them with you and loved how happy you were in those moments.

You won in the end. Later in life you were able to live clean and simple, without psychiatric drugs. You did it on your own terms, with the right diet, exercise, vitamins and minerals and control of your environment, by setting it up like only an engineer could, in a way that was optimum for your survival. You proved them all wrong and so many others who judged you as insane and wrote you off.

In my fifties around the same age, I found myself in exactly the same situation as you. Alone and completely failed by the medical system, struggling with a hormone imbalance that no one seemed to have a solution for. Now I know we both had the same thing — a hormone imbalance along with mental health issues such as PTSD that were exacerbated by the hormone fluctuations beyond our control.! How crazy is that? Your hormone issue was insulin and mine was lack of oestrogen and progesterone which causes sleep deprivation and psychosis. This triggered our mental health issues and the outcome of that perfect storm was devastating over and over again.

I miss you not being here by my side, to give you the blow by blow of each fight and each victory. I know you are looking down on me, proud as punch saying, "That's my girl". Love you forever, Dad, until we meet again in a sweeter place, with a better future for us all.

This is for all those victims murdered by psychiatry. Who, like my father, suffered from the barbaric treatment of electroshock treatment that did nothing but erase his memory, ability, and caused his early death.

Just remember this: "they fry your brain, because they do not understand your mind". They have no solution but to destroy. One day we will win this war and those responsible will be held accountable for their actions. For they do know what they do.

My mother: Has not had an easy life. Surviving domestic violence was something that changed her forever but not in a bad way. My mother is the strongest person I know and the most loving. She is the perfect mix of compassion, kindness, boundaries and tenacity. I am very like her in so many ways in her directness, intelligence and ability to survive and adapt to life's curve balls. Through her life she suffered greatly due to my father, and she has never been able to forgive him which is understandable. It is only when I look back, and realise she was so young, trying to handle so much that I can fully understand the decisions she had to make when we were small.

Today I am so lucky that I have such a close and loving relationship with my mother who has been there for me one hundred percent through this whole journey. I was fortunate that she is medically minded and understood that my problems were mainly hormonal. The biggest gift she gave me was to understand how serotonin depletion during menopause was adding to my problems. Serotonin depletion is triggered by crashing oestrogen which happens after childbirth and during menopause, in fact it can impact a woman's mind so severely that she can end up a suicide case, it is that serious. Serotonin is the feel-good hormone and without it life can get pretty dark and it stuns me that no medical professional ever even mentioned the word. There was never a doubt my mother would be there for me, no matter what and today as we look back it is our triumph that I have come through this strong, healthy and happy. So, I thank her from the bottom of my heart for doing what no one else could and that is loving me unconditionally whilst I worked out how to love myself. By loving myself enough I am conquering an ongoing menopausal battle that will not end but can be manageable.

3

A Childhood Survived

I was born in a small country village, called Istead Rise in England in a newly built house surrounded by apple orchards and cherry trees. It sounds idyllic and in many ways it was. I had an older brother and sister, Marc and Kay, and I was the third born and then my brother Steven came along a few years later. My father, Tony Wadham, was a hard-working, extremely clever engineer. He was mathematically a genius and very early on it was recognized and accepted that he would go far, and he did, being the chief designer and inventing the drill that created the passenger tunnels at Gatwick Airport for British Airways Authority.

My father had many health issues throughout his life that started when he became an insulin-dependent diabetic aged nineteen and it changed his life forever. The common solution back then, was for the doctor to prescribe lithium. Definition: the lightest known metal, can also lighten your mood. Lithium, atomic number three, is an element of many uses. I can only imagine what taking this toxic drug was like and know it created a perfect storm with his mental health.

He was a complicated man for sure, with a short fuse and a love of boxing. Nothing he loved more than proving himself against an opponent and there was no shortage of guys that came down from the Old Kent Road, in London, to beat the man whose right hook was fast becoming a legend. The stories my dad and his brother, Uncle David, told would keep us all entertained for hours. We could not hear enough of how my dad was undefeated and a nuclear missile (literally with all that lithium running around inside him). The best part about it was my father just loved to fight, but his brother Uncle David was shrewder, and without my father knowing, he made bets on him winning and cleaned up every time. For my father, knocking people out was just something he was good at, plus it was good exercise and kept him in shape. You know that thing kids do in the playground when they brag "my dad can beat your dad", Well I had the dad that could actually back it up and he often did.

My parents met when they were very young and did what everyone else did during the post-war era, and that was to move out of Greater London, as quickly as possible. During the war, my father and his brothers had been evacuated and were protected from much of the bombing. This was not the same for girls; my mother still remembers the air raids they experienced on the outskirts of South London in Erith. During the war, girls tended to stay home as it was deemed safer for them, as my mother and her sister were so young. My mother still has so many stories of hearing the air raid sirens every night which was terrifying. If it was too late to get to a shelter then she was put in the cupboard under the stairs, with her sister Brenda until it had all passed.

Eventually it all ended, and everyone got back to living their lives and working hard to repair the damage which was catastrophic. Eventually my mum got her first job at fifteen years old, in a paint factory owned by Dennis Thatcher. This was years before his wife Margaret became prime minister. My mum had always loved working and was so happy to be contributing. It was very important to her to help her parents as much as she could. She even managed to save enough money for the deposit on my parents' first home.

As the date got closer to my parents' wedding, my mother was seriously having second thoughts. My dad was jealous, aggressive, violent, controlling and quite frankly, she was scared of him more than she was in love with him. So often they would be walking down a street and another man would look at my mum a certain way and that was it; lights out, he would get belted, and the poor guy never even saw it coming. My dad did not tolerate anyone looking at my mother, for any reason, ever.

For my mum it was not possible to back out of the wedding; the social stigma and shame would have sent my grandparents over the edge for sure. It was just not an option. So, for my mum it was too late, and she did what was expected of that era. She got married. The wedding took place on 9th July 1960. My parents looked so happy in the photos, but behind the smiles there were secrets that no one was talking about. My mum wore a beautiful below-the-knee white dress she made herself. She had copied the style from a picture of Brigitte Bardot she found in a magazine and my dad stood there, head up, chest out, looking so proud. She really was a beauty. It was magical for a moment or two.

Shortly after the wedding, they set off for a holiday in Spain and their mode of transport was my father's Ducati motorbike. It was pretty crazy, but they were young, excited and on a budget, so they would make it work. Considering he was a diabetic and on lithium, it was pretty dangerous looking back, but she was good at managing his blood sugar for him and had no problem just shovelling food into his helmet the whole way through Europe.

Once back and moved into their new home, life settled down and within two years my mother got pregnant with my brother Marc. My mum was obsessed with babies, so she could not wait to start a family but once pregnant she was totally bored and hated sitting at home waiting, so at eight months pregnant she landed a temporary job working in London at the National Gallery. She spent her days enjoying paintings and Italian marble sculptures and when she was at home, she was knitting baby clothes like mad. It was her happiest time. As the birth date of my brother got closer, she reluctantly gave up her job at the gallery and stayed at home to nest.

When Marc was born, he was a big, beautiful, bonny baby, who looked like an angel. Before they knew it my parents were pregnant again, this time with my sister Kay, who turned out to be a dark-haired, brown-eyed beauty, with a twinkle in her eye. She was the mini-me of my father. I would love to have thought life was good for them, but frankly nothing could be further from the truth. My parents fought a great deal, and anything could set my father on edge. He had zero tolerance or patience and way before I was even born it was a very unhappy marriage.

They had one more child after me, my younger brother Steven, who was just adorable. For some reason, my mother kept putting him in dresses, red velvet ones that were beautiful. Apparently, that is how you dressed boy babies back then or, so we were told. We still give him stick for it. Whilst my dad was at work my mum often took us over to see our grandparents for the afternoon. My grandad was fun and silly, and it was a familiar place that had rose wallpaper going up the stairs to the bathroom and the smell of cooking always wafting around. It was very much a safe haven.

Every Christmas we would end up with my grandparents, which was always a treat, as it kept my father on good behaviour for a short time. I loved being around my extended family especially when my great great-uncle Peter would come down from Hyde Park, where he lived and play with us for hours. He would love to hold me up in the air and fly me around the room like a plane and I would scream with laughter. Considering I was pretty chubby back then I was lucky I did not get dropped on my head! He was very glamorous and had spent his life travelling and seeing the world, which was very exciting back in those days, because hardly anyone in my family had been anywhere, unless it was to fight for their country. After the war, Uncle Peter had been the valet for a physician called Lord Moran, who was the private doctor of Winston Churchill from 1940, until the great man's death on 24th January 1965. My uncle travelled with Lord Moran and Winston to some pretty amazing places and always had incredible stories and souvenirs. My family was very proud of him. When I was born on 31st March 1965, three months after Winston's death the news of my arrival certainly cheered Uncle Peter up tremendously.

As I grew up, home was never a safe place to be. It was somewhere to be in hiding. My mother protected us as much as she could and kept us out of the way so we did not set my dad on edge when he returned home from work, as he would be hungry and irritable. The favourite expression in those times was "children should be seen and not heard". Quite frankly I didn't want to be seen at all and spent a great deal of my life up in my room secretly wishing I was invisible. I grew up listening to shouting, screaming and fighting. We were all utterly terrified of my father and his tyrannic temper.

When I look back at our childhood pictures, we look terrified in every shot. One particular photo we have is of us all, that my mum took in the front garden of our village house by the willow tree, and we look absolutely petrified and that was exactly the reality of the situation. A picture paints a thousand words for sure, especially in this case as we were standing next to my father looking like scared rabbits. It was never a good thing to be anywhere near his right hook or his left for that matter, he was just so quick.

We all got very good at keeping out of my father's way. I figured out quickly not to stand too close to him, so I didn't catch the full force of a blow if he suddenly lashed out because I made a mistake. I also figured out the rough length of his right arm and how many feet that was when fully stretched and that is where I would stand, at the very end point of that measurement. Just slightly out of reach so he would have to move his body to reach me and then I could counter and move backwards. These were the kind of survival lessons a child should not have to learn at five years old, but I caught on quickly and that was my saving grace.

As time went by, I realised I was developing hyper-vigilance and started to see things before they happened, which I thought was normal. I would see a scene play out in full colour and sound and then later that day exactly what I had visualised happened right in front of me. I just assumed everyone was able to predict the future; it became my normal and is true for kids being raised in danger and violence. When it is not safe to speak, for the sound might give away your location, you learn to communicate with your siblings on a higher plane. Marc, Kay, Steven and I could read each other's minds. With just a look the four of us could say everything that was needed such as "Dad's home", "lie low", "keep quiet", "stay down" and so much more. You became so in tune with each other, the bond is tremendously strong as you depend on each other for safety and survival.

As the years went by, we were like so many dysfunctional families, in that what goes on behind closed doors stays there. We looked like the perfect family of successful and beautiful parents. We had gorgeous clothes, all handmade by my talented mother on her sewing machine. Our hair was perfectly groomed and styled, except for when Mum went too mad with the scissors, cutting our fringe so that we ended up looking like kids in a concentration camp! That was not fun for sure. The neighbours, of course, heard my mother's screams and saw her broken and bruised body, but they were powerless to do anything about it. My mother would call the police, who would arrive and see the damage and literally said their hands were tied because domestic violence was not recognized in those days. It was madness. She even asked the vicar of our local church to come and speak to my father, but he just kicked him out and told him to mind his own business, so that was that, there was nothing she could do to change the situation.

Then one day it all changed, and it was a shock for sure. For me, it was just another day, walking home from school in the sunshine, at six years old. As I went down the front garden path, I had to duck from being hit with the branches of a big and beautiful willow tree; it had grown so much since I was a baby. I took my time, as usual, because who wanted to rush home to that big mess and school was the only reprieve we had from fear and chaos.

Strangely, I noticed my dad's white Ford Cortina was parked in the driveway. Him being home early was not a good sign. As I walked around the back of the house, through the wooden country gate and into the kitchen, he was standing there with my mother's friend Pat. Apparently, they were now together, and we were told our mother was never coming back and that was that.

We were not sure if this was true as we had seen her pack her suitcase before and leave, many, many times over the years. I would often just watch her from the window as she walked to the bus stop in the village, keeping her in my sight until she was gone. Her long, beautiful hair hanging down her back, beautifully dressed but totally broken. It was a normal operating basis for us, but this day felt different. Needless to say, it was devastating when we realised she was never going to live with us again and our lives had just changed forever and gone with her was any love and protection we had ever known. We now had to get used to a new normal and the survival stakes had just gone up.

In some ways this new system was better as instead of coming straight home from work hungry, tired and mean, my dad would go to Pat's house to eat. She only lived down the street, so they could have romantic, undisturbed dinners together, without a bunch of kids around. Of course, we were never invited and would come home from school ravenous and just make do with whatever we could find. The downside to that deal was there was never much in the fridge. Not because my father could not afford it, but because he didn't give it much thought. I remember beating egg whites for hours trying to make meringues to put in the oven as I was so hungry, but it was so much work I gave up in the end. Being hungry was the new normal as well.

As potential 'future stepmums' go, Pat was pretty terrible. She had no children of her own, barely communicated unless she was being mean and had no interest in us. She did not make herself very popular by constantly telling us off in front of my dad, who would then stop what he was doing, join in and back her up. It was as if she enjoyed winding him up and watching us suffer because of it. She was the worst and we hated her.

Occasionally, whilst we were at school she would come to the house and snoop around. She would go through our bedrooms and scold us for how messy we were. My sister Kay was livid once when she came home from school one day and found her underwear hanging up at the window. Pat had decided that was the way to teach children to pick up their dirty clothes from the floor. Literally the whole street could see my sister's knickers at the window. What a bitch! Who does that? We hated her even more. My mum would never have done that.

If we were lucky now and then we would see mum on the weekend or if she could, she would pop in at teatime on her break from her new job as a delivery driver. Our stolen time with her was always so precious. My mum would have loved to have taken us with her when she left. It absolutely broke her not being able to, but during that time, there were no shelters for abused women, especially ones with four kids in tow. She was told she would be given somewhere in a few weeks but that turned into six years and a massive court case for custody of us all that my father was determined to win at any cost. Life was shit to say the least.

As most kids do in these situations, we soon figured out how to get through each day. If we did our daily chores and kept out of the way, we could dodge a good hiding. God help the poor bugger who was first to be called downstairs when my father came home from work; it did not mean anything good. It meant you had not completed your chores properly and were in some trouble. We suffered in silence and had no help from anyone; no friends, family or neighbours, even though everyone knew what was going on. Not even the school teachers could help us and to be honest they didn't care either. When our aunts and uncles tried to help us, my father stopped them from coming over. It was that simple. He had all the control. There are times I can still remember sitting on the staircase at home listening to my mother screaming, begging him to stop. The only good thing that came out of mum not living with us any more, was not hearing her cries after yet another beating.

I cried for my mother almost every day; we all did. Most weekends I would quietly sit in my room and play a record by Jimmy Osmond called 'Mother of Mine' and sob. I felt so very sorry for myself and would make it worse by playing the song over and over and over and then sit by the window, waiting for her to come back. I honestly believe I developed a longing, craving for love at this point.

There were some good times now and then for sure, like occasionally we were allowed to see our cousins from my father's side of the family. Maria and Lisa would come over with their parents, my Uncle David and Auntie Madeleine, and a good day would be had by all. It was as if everything was perfect and we were a normal family for one day, as my father could relax and enjoy his brother's conversations. This was a welcome distraction, as he was not so focused on every little thing we did wrong. This was always such a relief. The kids would all play upstairs and listen to the Bay City Rollers, dance and jump on the bed. My Uncle David was the only male adult I was not afraid of and so many times I wished he had been my father.

My grandparents would visit now and then and bring home-made treacle toffee (we kind of dreaded it as it was so bitter, and you usually would end up with a broken tooth or two). There were times of respite during my childhood, but they were too few and far between.

I remember very clearly one particular Sunday I was helping my sister make Sunday lunch by peeling the potatoes and I was running hot water to keep my hands warm, instead of using cold water, as my dad had always instructed us. He absolutely hated waste of any kind and even inspected the peelings to make sure they were not too thick; you get very skilled with a knife under those circumstances. I knew it was a bad idea wasting hot water like this, but I did it anyway thinking I could get away with it. Sunday was also car wash day and my brothers usually got roped in to help my dad clean the car. He absolutely loved his cars; they were his pride and joy. I was very alert to the fact that he may need to come in and get some more water, so I had my wits about me as usual but somehow, I got distracted talking to my sister and the next thing I knew my dad was up close and looking right at me. It was not a big kitchen and I instinctively moved away but as I turned, he noticed I was wearing a necklace and asked me where I had got it from. I never wore jewellery of any kind or make-up; it was a definite no-no in our house. I told him my mum had given it to me earlier in the week and knew before the words were even out of my mouth I was in danger.

Cornered between the sink and the counter space there was no escape, there never was. His hand came towards me so fast; I did not even have time to duck. I felt him going for my throat and the necklace was ripped from my neck as he violently snapped the chain. Once it was in his grip he turned and walked away, leaving the back of my neck bleeding and me, as usual cowering on the floor crying. This tended to be my usual position after he had finished his punishment. Most times I would wet myself in pure terror, but I had learned if I did that, I would be in for even more punishment for making a mess on the carpet. He had made his point this time and walked back to the kitchen door that led to the garden and calmly turned around and said, "You may look like your mother, but if you ever grow up like her, I will kill you". I did not doubt it for one second as I had seen first-hand what he had done to her in the past.

The next day his solution for me looking like my mum, was to give me a home haircut. I had this long, crazy, blonde, curly mess of ringlets that had a life of its own. I so wanted to look less like Shirley Temple (which was my dad's nickname for me) and more like the girls at school, with their long, straight, swingy hair, hanging down their backs as mine just grew straight up like Marge Simpson's, but less blue thankfully. As he stood me in the bathtub I shivered as he came towards me with a big pair of scissors and tried to stand still as he cut my hair over my ears and straight across the back. I now resembled a grubby homeless child, and it was a disaster for sure as once my hair was dry it bounced up even higher and I looked like an onion head. It was so short; I could not even put it in a ponytail to hide how horrible it was. I cried for days. If I had felt like an ugly duckling before, it was now confirmed. I was the ugliest kid on the planet, and no one would ever love me. It felt like I really could not catch a break.

My siblings did not fare much better. We were all living in terror and dreaded the end of each workday as we waited for his car to pull into the drive. My younger brother Steven was only four years old and the baby still, so we all pulled together to protect him at every chance we could. Most of the time we were successful but there were times he slipped through the safety net of our love and got himself into trouble. It was awful when that happened.

Once he was so hungry, he went to the fridge and bit into a lump of cheese and put it back with the teeth marks still in it, or we assumed it was him. Of course, he did not think to use a knife or cover his teeth marks; he was a little child. When my father found the cheese later that night, he lined us up and asked who did it. No one stepped forward, we just stood there in silence. My father told us if the guilty person did not step forward, he would not punish us all. We stood there terrified to move and then out of the left corner of my eye I saw Steven as he stepped forward and said he did it. It was sickening watching him being punished but that was my dad's way of keeping us in line; we had to watch. If I had known Steven was going to make a move, I would have stepped forward instead, but I didn't see it play out and punished myself for not protecting him. I would have preferred to have taken the beating myself, rather than watch this little boy crying and taking the punishment of a man. I found out years later it was not even him that bit into the cheese; he just did not want to see any of us get hurt. That is how strong our bond was, completely unbreakable. To this day it still is.

There were no favourites in our household, and no one got off lightly. It was hell for all of us, but we just got through it, praying one day it would be over. I just hoped we prayed loud enough, so God could hear us, but quietly enough so my father could not. As the divorce battle raged on, my mother desperately fought for our freedom in court.

After one long day in court my dad came home and called us all downstairs. Apparently, the judge had sent my father home to question us on who we wanted to live with. Were they completely fucking crazy? Did they really think we felt safe enough to tell him we would rather die than live with him? He lined us up, as usual, like little military soldiers and stood there with his girlfriend Pat as he asked each of us the dreaded question in turn, "Who do you want to live with, me or your mother?" Of course, I lied and said we wanted to live with him. I may have been scared but I was not stupid. Marc and Steven both followed me, and lied and said the same just to stay safe. Then it was Kay's turn. She stepped forward and said she wanted to live with our mum. We were all shocked. In my mind I was willing her to take it back, to change her mind, say something else or just bloody run. But she was not tuning in to my thoughts; she was just staring straight up at him in defiance which made him even worse. She could see how angry he was and then she took it one step further and said, "Go on then, hit me, I know you are going to anyway." She had reached the point of no return. That moment when you know you have nothing left to lose and would not succumb any more.

I have never seen anyone so brave in my life. Of course, she got whacked for giving him 'lip' and as we all knew he would, the judge awarded my father custody, and our fate was sealed. I know my dad did not really want us; he was just hell bent on not letting my mother win, but at the end of the day it just didn't matter any more.

I tried to tell myself it was not his fault, as I loved him so much. I justified it with the fact that his temper would get the better of him or his reactions were too quick for him to catch, or he was not well due to his diabetes, because I didn't just have bad memories, I had incredible ones as well and I didn't want them lost forever. Like when he got me my first bike and taught me to ride it. I remember it like it was yesterday. I was so happy when he pushed me down the road and promised to not let go as I was only learning and of course he let go and I flew all by myself. It was an incredible moment and as I looked back to see what happened to him, he was proud as punch, laughing so hard at the surprised look on my face. We were both beaming from ear to ear. Like most children, my bike became my world. It was the first taste of freedom and a new form of escape, other than my legs.

During the long hot summer breaks from school, I could stay out on my bike all day and never get tired of it. I would ride round and round the village like a crazy chicken, never getting tired of the same small route. I just wanted to go again and again and try to count and time myself to see how fast I was and if I was getting faster. The feeling of freedom was amazing and clearly, I was in love with my bike, but there was still something missing in my life for sure as what I really wanted was a pony.

The total highlight of my childhood was our horse riding lessons at Tollgate Riding Stables on Sunday mornings. I would be so excited I could barely breathe, and my dad could see I was getting overwhelmed and make me stop, take a breath and calm down before I passed out! I just took life's wins as huge victories and found it hard to keep all that energy in my little body; it wanted to rush out all at once if I was too happy. Crazy that I thought there was such a thing as being too happy, but apparently there is. My excitement sometimes got me into far worse trouble than my inner rebel ever did.

The stables were only a ten-minute drive so dad would pile us all in the car and we were all geared up and were raring to go. We all had our favourite pony who we rode every time if we got there first and put dibs on him, or her and for me it was Apollo. He was jet black and just like the horse in the movie *National Velvet* with Elizabeth Taylor. I had watched it so many times and wanted to be a jockey just like her. Apollo was huge, or at least he was to me, as I was not very big at the time. In reality he was just a little, shaggy pony that liked me and made my life complete for an hour every Sunday. During our lessons, my father would stand outside the freezing cold arena, watching us intently, taking photos, waving and smiling as we bobbed around in a circle showing off for him. He absolutely loved the trip as much as we did. On one of those outings, he told us horse poop is fertiliser and makes things grow, so from then on, my sister Kay and I stood in it at every chance we got. We wanted to grow tall and get to adulthood faster. Looking back, it is so funny how kids take things so literally. On a recent trip down memory lane with my brother, Marc, he told me that when our boots were muddy my father would drive home and make us walk miles in the pouring rain, funny how I did not remember this and tended to make my father the hero when the opposite was true.

My dream of my own pony was never going to be a reality as our garden was too small, so I decided the only thing to do was make one myself and miraculously I managed to turn my bike into a pony/bike. I got my hands on my dad's thin garden twine and a tape measure. I measured how long the string needed to be and tied the ends to each of the handlebars. This was genius, as it left the loop in the middle to be used as reins, to make steering possible. Off I went down the road, so proud of myself that I could now practise my rising trot manoeuvres and did not have to wait for Sunday riding lessons to come. My plan was to practise like mad on my bike and then by the time I jumped on Apollo, my trot would be perfect, and my dad would be amazed that his daughter was such a talented future Olympic champion. That is kind of how my mind worked back then, still does if I am honest.

Everything was going to plan, practising my trotting every day until the inevitable happened and I picked up a little too much speed, lost control of my 'reins' and slammed into a curb. As I flew over the top of the handlebars, everything went into slow motion. It was like flying, which made me laugh for a split second, thinking wow, this is even better; I now have to get an airplane too which was great until I hit the ground and smashed one of my front teeth through my lip and chipped it in the process.

With blood pouring down my face, from a split lip, the fun had come to a rather abrupt halt. Fortunately, my dad was home, as it was the weekend, and my sister Kay ran to tell him I had died on my bike; she was very dramatic back then but to be honest I did look like a horror show. My dad came sprinting down the street and picked me up from the hard ground, hugging me to make me feel better. I covered his lovely shirt in blood, and I am pretty sure he was practically deaf from me screaming blue murder in his ears, but he did not care. It was pretty awful except for one valuable lesson I learned which is this: my dad loves me; this was proof of that love, and it made me feel happy. A seed had been planted in my mind that when I hurt myself, he proves how much he cares. That cognition would backfire on me later in life for sure as I went through relationships hurting myself to get someone to prove their love for me. Thankfully those days are well and truly over.

Clearly, I was banned by my father from ever using the pony/bike trick again. I had scared him to death with that stunt. Knowing how it ended with me bleeding and screaming you would think I would be just fine with that, but oh no, I was not going to let a flying lesson stop me. I was so wilful, stubborn and just obsessed with conquering this manoeuvre, there was no way I was going to stop trying. I just got smarter and did it during the week instead. My smart dad caught on and was always one step ahead; the garden string disappeared, which put an end to my antics.

The chaos in my home life was never mentioned out loud by anyone, ever. At our local school no one seemed to care what our lives were like, even though they had all been informed my mother was no longer living at home and was not to be called if we were sick or needed picking up. We had a very strict teacher called Mrs Rose, who was a chubby woman with brown, curly hair that stuck out everywhere. She clearly went to the hairdresser once a week to get it done as it never, ever moved, not even once. It always looked the same. She taught the music class once a week and as my dad loved music, jazz especially, he had high hopes that one of us would turn out to be musically minded, but he was sadly disappointed. We were the most tone deaf, musically challenged kids in the village for sure, but lessons were compulsory, and I was very down to give it a go, I was so sure I had hidden talents somewhere.

On the first day of music class, we all had to choose which instrument we would play. This was a tough choice as I was sure I was talented at them all; delusional thinking clearly took hold early on in my life. I narrowed it down to the violin or the recorder and settled on the violin as it came with a carrying case which was the most important thing about learning a musical instrument. You would certainly get noticed for being musically talented carrying the case around if nothing else, regardless of whether you could play it or not. I proudly walked home from school later that afternoon, with my case on full display, excited to practise. I actually think, looking back, the feeling of carrying the case and looking special, far outweighed trying to play the horrible, squeaky thing. As it turned out, not surprisingly, I was absolutely terrible with the violin. The screeching noise from my bedroom was too much for anyone to cope with, let alone the neighbours, my siblings and my poor, stressed-out father, who was already at the end of his rope. He gently told me that he thought a recorder would be a better option for his up and coming musically talented daughter, because you could just carry it in your pocket so easily and you always knew where it was. Clearly, he didn't get the whole 'holding the case, walking home from school, looking special situation', but adults can be dumb like that sometimes I realized. I actually felt bad for him, so I agreed with him to change back to the recorder. I have never seen him so happy when I told him, however the stupid recorder landed me in even more trouble as it was so small and convenient, I kept losing it.

Keep in mind I am about nine years old now and have a lot on my plate already. I had no diary or schedule to remind me when the stupid lesson was going to be, so the recorder often got left at home when it was needed.

Of course, all the other kids had their mother at home doing everything for them and would look all perfect with their newly washed hair styled into pigtails as they excitedly whipped out their shiny black recorders and all started showing off playing *Three Blind Mice*. I just sat there like a lemon, thinking, oh shit, I wonder if Mrs Rose will notice. Another moment in my life that having a superpower like being invisible would have really come in handy.

When the eagle-eyed Mrs Rose spotted me sitting there, twiddling my thumbs, hoping the ground would swallow me she did not hold back. She told me I was not worth tuppence, in front of the whole class. She damn well knew I did not have a mum at home to remind me what day it was. I was lucky if I could find a matching pair of socks and get there on time let alone find a bloody stupid recorder. She shamed me and made me feel worthless in front of the whole class. I hated her. I hated school, I hated myself and my life. That kind of thinking stayed from then on out for many, many years. I harboured a resentment and hatred of teachers for the rest of my school life.

Weekends were not much better than school to be honest. The hardest part for us all was that my dad worked at home every weekend, so we all had to keep out of the way and stay quiet. He would bring home his huge blueprints from work and spread them out on the dining room table. Then he would move all the dining chairs back a few feet, so he could walk around and study his work from any angle. I would watch him for hours, happily in his zone, playing classical music and viewing from above, his penmanship whilst working on a strategy for solving mathematical problems. It looked really complex and demanded complete focus and concentration, but strangely it did not stress him out, like we did; it actually relaxed him. It seemed to take him to a higher place in his mind, where his demons would leave him in peace, and he could just be in the moment. Often, he would let me sit and watch him and he would explain what he was working on and the process of going through complex movements as he drew them and told me numbers never lie, people do. I am not sure I fully understood the meaning of it at the time, but later on, it would be a survival tool that would literally save me as during menopause I only trusted the numbers on my blood work, rather than the doctors moving their lips, feeding me bullshit.

As he worked, my father taught me the importance of setting up a desk before you begin. He showed me the importance of tool care and placement and how everything has a place and there is a place for everything. There were so many sayings he used as he tried to teach us how to be the very best in life. Putting things back where you found them was another big thing on his list; there was nothing worse than if we used the scissors and then did not put them back and he needed them. No one wanted to be in that position, especially with scissors involved.

He showed us all the importance of taking good care of our 'tools of the trade' as they are what made your job possible and how you earned money. He wanted us to understand why his pencils and pens were so important, as that is how he put food on the table and had a good job in life. It made sense for sure. Very methodically he would lay out all of his technical drawing instruments. They were meticulously placed, and every pencil was sharp and clean. His rulers, triangles and his compass (a tool that inscribes small circles or arcs), were all perfectly positioned, in the exact same place every time. That way he could work without stopping, automatically knowing exactly where something was without having to even look. It was a beautiful dance to behold, as he was truly in the moment and in his higher mind. I understand it much better now as I go through the writing process, which feels very similar. I need my system and routine, so I am not scrabbling around trying to find things and losing concentration.

Every now and then whilst watching my dad work, he would test my maths times tables which were terrible. It was always a nerve-racking moment, and my mind would go completely blank due to fear and panic. If I was not quick enough with the answer, it was bad, but if I guessed and got it wrong then that was worse. No matter what the good intention was of teaching me to do maths quickly, it backfired as I just could not learn under duress and fear. I shut down mentally the moment I was put on the spot. This is called PTSD (post-traumatic stress disorder), but of course that was not known back then. It was more associated with men coming back from the war but home life for some can be a war zone.

The simplest of questions could be overwhelming, as the fear of what could happen next overtook my mind and shut me down. Even if I knew the answer, I could not reach it fast enough. Usually, I would just stand there staring at him. On a good day I would just be called stupid and told to go away and on a bad day, if he was hungry and his blood sugar was low, he could fly off the handle and I would just cower in terror. He started off meaning so well, being a good dad and teaching me, but it went south fast, and he had no control over his temper due to his insulin crashing around him and the stress and overwhelm of what he was trying to do at that moment. Having now studied the hormone insulin I understand this is diabetic rage but as a child you do not have that information. In his work life, people's lives literally depended on him getting the numbers lined up and right. I had no concept of that as a child. I understand it more now having experienced the same overwhelm, with crashing blood sugar levels in menopause, due to low progesterone that controls blood sugar levels in the body.

Later on in life, I discovered that the hormone Progesterone has a great deal to do with diabetes, as it also controls insulin and can turn on the symptoms of diabetes, where you are literally hungry constantly, confused, anxious and stressed. I realized going through this myself, it is how it must have been for my dad. On days when my Progesterone is low, I am lucky if I can write a sentence that is readable, let alone design a complex drilling bit, like he did, that would become a pioneering design in engineering. My dad really was such an incredible engineer. It blows my mind when I look back as I remember him working away, quietly playing his classical music creating a masterpiece.

All the memories from my past, good and bad, form a melting pot of mixed emotions for me to sift through. Happiness, fear, pain, anger, apathy, anxiety and confusion all course through me as I revisit my childhood in my mind. The past has made a huge impact on who I am as a person and how I have navigated my life.

My dad did his best, that is for sure, but he had serious health issues with his diabetes that a child could never understand. For some he is the villain in my childhood, but not for me. I knew deep down he was a giant who was getting the shit kicked out of him by life. We had all seen him cry in absolute desperation and heartbreak the many times my mother left him. He struggled for years with his diabetes and on a regular basis he would fall into a coma and be carted off by an ambulance. Many times, we thought he was dead and just didn't know what to do, as we could not wake him up. Once the ambulance took him away, we would go to bed and know that he would be home tomorrow after he had some insulin and some rest. It was our normal and we saw his vulnerability as well as his demons and all had a love/hate thing going on for sure.

The amazing thing about life is that you never know when a miracle will happen, and they do happen every single day. I was thirteen years old when my miracle happened. Out of the blue, my father came home from work and told us all we were going to live with our mother. We stood there in absolute shock, knowing not to react in a happy way but to look a bit sad at the news. On the inside we were already celebrating, but cautious in case he changed his mind. He said he had had enough of us and that was it; the spell was broken, and we were free. God does work in mysterious ways. I have never believed this more than today, as I look back and realize the lessons my father taught me were impossible to live without.

My siblings and I could now leave this place, with all its memories and horrors and we would be starting a new life with my wonderful, loving, kind and patient mother. Looking back, it was literally like we were being let out of prison and I happily did not see my father again for ten years. To be honest I did not miss him at all during that time and I developed a saying that if I ever ran into him and he was on fire I would not even piss on him. That is how much hatred I had for him and thankfully, over time this opinion softened but for now we were all so lucky to be alive and needed time to heal.

Thankfully, my mother had never given up on us and she never lost hope of getting us to safety one day. She had the same prayers and the same goal and purpose in life, as we did; to get us home with her again. It took years but my God, it was worth the fight.

4

Ugly Duckling Broken Swan

It was a beautiful summer morning when my mum picked us all up in her car and drove us to our new home. I remember walking into the house for the first time and going up the staircase to my bedroom that I would share with my sister. It had been beautifully decorated with a beautiful blue paper that had white flowers on it and a spongy feel when you touched it. The ceilings were very high, and the room had beautiful sash windows with little square panes. It looked out onto the back garden that had a black iron gate leading out onto the alleyway at the back. This would be my escape route on my bike for years to come. It was a beautiful, safe and happy place called home. It was a dream come true; we could barely believe it.

Our new home was a three-story, Victorian semi on Peacock Street in a town called Gravesend. Having only lived in the countryside, moving into town was a culture shock to say the very least. It was on the River Thames, which was really exciting for us kids. I made friends quickly and spent hours wading through mud to swim in the water over the summer. I probably had toxic poisoning by the time autumn came but didn't care one bit. I don't think I saw my brother Marc much for the first year; he was the eldest and he was off racing around on his bike having a blast every day. He had the same bike obsession as I did and could even fix his bikes himself, which always impressed me. We were all bouncing off the walls with excitement because for the first time ever we were loved, safe, provided for and could sleep peacefully without fear.

My mother wisely made the decision that we would not change schools and would commute to the countryside daily as she knew we had already been through enough. It took months before I was able to take in the enormity of our life change. Nightmares would haunt me and sometimes I would wake up in a hot sweat thinking I was back with my dad. Eventually those nightmares stopped, and we overcame the trauma that living in fear had impinged upon us.

Our finances were very different after the move, as we had zero financial assistance from my father. When I think now that my mum was only thirty-five years old, it blows my mind to realize how young she was handling all of this. She worked multiple jobs to feed us and put clothes on our backs. God only knows how she juggled it all but there was always a hot meal on the table, food in the fridge and our clothes were always clean and ironed. We had gone from having to do everything for ourselves to really enjoying doing absolutely nothing to help if we could get away with it.

This financial change was the first time I noticed we were different from my school friends, and I started to feel very self-conscious that I could not afford to do the same things as they could. My clothes were not cool and if we wanted to go on a day out, I did not have money to spend like they did. To me it was very noticeable and very embarrassing at times. I guess I learned along the way that having no money was something to be ashamed of and meant you were literally worthless. It seemed the pennies in your purse were calculated by others, as a direct relation to your worth as a human being. No money equals worthless. I had finally got good at maths, and it did not feel good at all.

I would shoplift as a kid, stupid things like make-up from Woolworths; it gave me a high when I got away with it. It kind of became the thing to do on a Saturday afternoon for fun. On one particular day, I got arrested for shoplifting a pair of jeans for my friend and as I ran out of the store, the shopkeeper started shouting at me and I slammed straight into a policeman, who grabbed me by the scruff of my neck and stopped me in my tracks. I felt like Oliver Twist, the street urchin, all grubby and angry and as hard as I could I sunk my teeth into him and kicked him in the shins, but he had a firm grip and marched me to the police station. Terrified my mother would go mad when she found out, I sat there refusing to give out my name.

Eventually, as they knew I would, I got cold and hungry which overtook the fear of my mother's reaction, and I gave them my address. When my mother arrived, she was mortified at my behaviour. She quickly realized that the jeans I had stolen were actually four sizes too big for me and I admitted they were for my new buddy. I was not allowed to see that friend again, as clearly, I was being badly influenced. It was actually the complete opposite way around, but I kept that to myself as it was my get out of jail free card. I would often bump into the bobby on the street as I grew up and he would smile and give me pep talks and ask me if I was behaving myself which of course I was, theoretically.

As I got older, I could never talk about money or admit it if I was broke, it was so humiliating. I hated it and wanted to be equal to those around me and not feel like a piece of garbage. All my friends in school seemed to be living good lives, their parents were married, not divorced which also set me apart. They did not have to line up and give special bright, red-coloured discs out for their school lunch; they had money to pay for it. Whoever thought this was a good system had clearly not been in that position themselves as children, as you could not miss the red discs; no one could. My shame was so strong that some days I would go without lunch rather than face the humiliation of busting out a disc.

My sister always knew when I was stressed; I would twirl my curly blonde ringlets for hours and it drove her mad. She was eighteen months older than me, and she had poker-straight dark hair that I always wanted, and she had huge brown eyes and was just so pretty. She looked just like my dad. She even had boys asking her out and no one even noticed I existed. In fact, I often got mistaken for a boy, which made sense as I was always climbing trees and had given up gymnastics for karate, which I was always practising at any given opportunity. Scrapping with my new townie friends became a game of survival of the fittest and although I was small, I often surprised them by being pretty tough.

I continued to commute to my old school in Meopham daily from town and had friends there but kept out of the way as much as I could as I hated school. To add to my embarrassment of struggling financially, I had made a new friend whose mother found out I lived in Gravesend and what a big difference that five miles made in the eyes of other people. I had only just moved there but as far as she was concerned, I was not good enough for her daughter. I soon ended up with the cruel nickname of 'That Ann'. I was not allowed to go to my friend's house or hang out with her any more and we were banned from being friends but that did not stop us. We would sneak around, but always got caught out in the end, but we never gave up.

Often, I would try and call my best friend from the phone box on the weekend to see if we could meet up and I had to pretend to be someone else if her mother answered, but I never got away with it, because her mother always knew it was me and slammed the phone down. I felt like a piece of garbage, ashamed of who I was and where I lived which was not good enough, even though to me it was the first time I had ever felt safe, and I loved my home. I was constantly reminded that I was nothing and now so filled with self-loathing that I started to take karate very seriously. I just had to get the anger out and beating the shit out of someone in a dojo was very therapeutic indeed.

In school I started to get in even more trouble with this rebellious streak seeping out of me. I was always trying to find mischief. I would do stupid things like jump across the desks in the break at school or deliberately let the locusts out of their cage in the science lab with my best friend, so they could fly around the room free. The other kids would all be screaming and diving under their desks as I ran to the door and locked them all in there.

I would skip class, hide in the bathroom and give my maths teacher a ton of backchat. I had zero respect for him. What did he know about maths and teaching, as clearly I did not understand a word he was saying. I now look back and realize children who are having serious problems at home act out at school to try and get attention, but it backfired on me many times. My teachers did not have any insight into my life and just thought I was a nightmare and warned other parents not to let their kids hang out with me, which in hindsight was understandable.

The school knew I had changed from living with my father, to now being with my mother, but before that change, my head teacher, Mr Eagles, gave me a really hard time about not submitting my report card, which was due back to the school on the Monday morning, signed by my dad. He accused me of not showing it to my father and he made me stand up in front of the class and called me a liar. Later that day he came up to me, having spoken to my father at work and he apologized for his mistake. Would have been nice if he had done that as publicly as he had humiliated me. My lack of respect for teachers did not improve at this point.

By now it was not that I didn't know right from wrong — I did — but honestly, I just didn't give a shit and wanted to test the boundaries and see what I could get away with. I had hardened to life and all I wanted to do was to fight, hence an obsession with karate, so I could take down anyone who threatened me in the future. I wanted to be a badass street kid and was happiest as a tomboy running around this new town of mine that I called home. Getting into mischief, swinging from the top of lamp posts at night, climbing trees, fighting the local kids or pelting people with snowballs from the rooftops were just a part of the fun. Knock down ginger became a great pastime, with so many town houses and places to hide. Bless my poor mother, she did not know half of what I got up to.

I believe it was during this time I was around sixteen and I started to become curious about boys. We had a local military school in the town and the boys would all stand around town near the phone boxes at night making calls to their families. We called them Peanuts; I still have no idea why but found out if you got dressed up and walked by the phone boxes, they would whistle. Now this was both terrifying and fascinating. I had started to grow up and I was curious about this thing called love! It was everywhere: my sister was in and out of love, the girls in my school were always falling in love, but it completely eluded me. What the hell was going on? Why was I different? Where was my love? Dammit, I was going to find some love somewhere even if it killed me.

One day my sister finally took pity on me, as I was a total tomboy and had no idea what I was doing with clothes and make-up, so she offered to help out mainly because she needed someone to go to a local disco with her and she chose me, as it was a Sunday night and none of her friends were allowed out. Without much persuasion needed I let her get me dolled up to go out for the first time. It was beyond exciting. She did my hair and make-up, squeezed me into some black stretchy pants and then lent me some high heels that did not fit that well, but we figured out I could walk in them if we stuffed some tissue down into the toes. I had a black and white striped sweater on and looked a bit like a mod, which was a good look back then, much better than being a rocker.

We were soon ready, with a ton of my mum's hairspray and perfume and off we went. On the way to the disco, I soon realized it was a bloody long walk for a girl in skin-tight trousers and tissue-stuffed shoes, but the excitement was overwhelming, and I was willing to suffer for beauty, in search of the love that was overdue and owed to me. As soon as we arrived, a good-looking boy came over to us. It was someone my sister knew, and he looked very cool in a Hugh Grant floppy hair kind of way. He asked my sister who I was and before I knew it, she had gone and I was being chatted up, which was amazing, until he tried to kiss me. To be honest, it was grossly uncomfortable, a bit like being slobbered on by a Great

Dane. I had no idea what I was doing, and my sister got me the hell away from him, what a creep. If this was love you could shove it; I would rather have a fight.

Other than the horrible kiss, the night was incredible; it was beyond anything I had ever experienced. My sister and I danced, drank cokes and I thought I was pretty cool as I carefully studied the crowd, always making sure I was safe. I watched how people moved and danced to the music and I tried to copy the cooler people, but I probably just looked like I was having a seizure, as I was a super geek to the max for sure.

The walk home went quickly, and we laughed as we recalled the events of the night. Of course, we were later home than our ten o'clock curfew and got busted, but it was the beginning of being grown up and I loved it. I swear my mother had radar ears, as even when we took our damn shoes off two miles away and walked barefoot home, she would still hear us. My God, you could just not get anything by this woman as she would be standing there at the door, with her curlers in and a grumpy, tired expression on her face, bless her. Fortunately, I did not have any more kissing incidents for a while, which I was quite happy with, and it stayed that way for a bit longer until the night I met my first love, or so I naively thought.

I was on a rare night out with my new karate friend Theresa. We were going to a pub in West Kingsdown as she was dating someone called Bob and I, as per usual, was single. Some other friends were with us, and we all had a few drinks and were having a nice evening when I noticed the guy behind the bar was literally staring me down. It was intense to say the least. He came over to the table once or twice and was a lot older than me but seemed very keen to speak to me. I was still only sixteen and not used to any attention from men, so it was a little unnerving at first. He introduced himself to the group, his name was Colin.

As the evening went on, I was totally flattered by Colin's attention, especially when he told us all he was not actually a bartender, he was a Formula Ford racing driver. He would be Formula 3 next year hopefully and he even had his own race car. He was good looking, skinny, and the only off-putting thing for me was that he had a moustache that looked like a dead mouse across his top lip; it was gross. I was not that impressed, but he would not stop talking to me and staring. At the end of the evening, I was flattered that he wrote his number on a piece of paper and gave it to me. His eyes literally bore into my soul, and I was torn between fear and curiosity but mostly I felt relief that someone was finally noticing me, it had been a long time coming. Having read way too many romantic novels by then, I was starting to wonder if this was my first love. My 'rose-coloured goggles' kicked in and I started to picture myself with this almost famous, moustache-sporting, super good-looking, uber cool, race car driver, who was slightly older than me and cooler than the silly boy who had tried to kiss me. I had no concept at the time that this age difference was very inappropriate and no idea that he was actually thirty-six years old. My need and desperation for attention and to be noticed far outweighed any common sense at this age. I honestly just didn't have any when it came to love and was totally out of my depth trying to figure it all out. In years to come I found this was a common pattern of mine: I would ignore the warning signs, no matter how blatant they were and just see what I wanted to see. It cost me a great deal in life doing relationships this way.

Back at the pub, I had butterflies. I could barely look at Colin without blushing, my heart took a leap, and I knew this was what I had been looking for — this was love at last! I had never had a boyfriend to compare anything to and was still a virgin which was embarrassing as all of my friends had very successfully gotten rid of their virginity. I was still intact at the grand old age of sixteen, which looking back is exactly how it should have remained.

Colin planned to take me out that weekend and said he would come and pick me up at my home in Gravesend. This was such a nerve-racking experience, especially since I had never had anyone come to my home before and as the day loomed closer, I felt a sick nervousness come over me. The fear of actually going on a date was overwhelming, which was strange, as it was everything I had wanted for so long and now I was just wracked with insecurities and self-loathing, knowing I did not have a fancy house like my friends and feeling ashamed of where I lived. I was not sure what would be worse, him turning up or not turning up.

Eventually the day was upon me and exactly on time the doorbell rang, and my mother went to the door. Of course, I heard it but wanted to look cool and not rush downstairs straight away; I wanted to make the right entrance. My mum came back from the door looking confused and said someone must be playing 'silly buggers' as there was no one there. This was really odd, so I went outside to look down the street and there was Colin standing three houses down hiding. He walked towards me and smiled. He explained that he was nervous my mum would open the door and he was scared to meet her due to his age. Red flag right there and I missed it completely. Even he knew how inappropriate this was, which makes it even worse as I look back. This was not illegal, but it was totally wrong. If anyone had told me how wrong it was, I would not have listened and I had no father around to tell him to 'sling his hook'.

The date went well, and we had something to eat. He had a little red sports car which was so fun, and he obviously drove it really fast which was exciting. We started to see each other regularly and although my mother initially had some serious reservations about the age difference, he was a gentleman and seemed very genuine and caring. She just wanted to make sure I finished my college course and didn't get carried away. Of course, both my mother and I were swept up in his charm and good looks at the time. She was pretty smitten and just happy I was happy.

Things started to take a turn for the worse when I started ducking out of college and eventually, we slept together, it is not something I can even remember and must have blanked it out. At that time, I had no idea he was a heavy drinker because he hid it so well in the beginning. Soon it was spring, and my birthday was upon us. I would be seventeen and Colin's family wanted to have a little get-together for me, with some cards and cake. I had not met his sisters before and wanted them to like me but then Colin told me I have to tell them I was eighteen and lie about my age. It was so uncomfortable as the birthday cards all had 'Happy 18th Birthday' on them and it was just a total lie. I was so nervous to even speak, in case I said the wrong thing, but everyone seemed really nice and thankfully we left after tea, and I could take a deep breath. I was a terrible liar and felt sure they all knew.

My father always said to be a good liar you need a good memory, and I just didn't have one of those, or so I thought. After my birthday Colin wanted to get engaged. We were in love and that was the next step and I agreed even though in the back of my mind I was feeling very uneasy, but I also thought that is what you did when you were in a physical relationship with a man. You got married. So, we got engaged, against my mother's wishes and I dropped out of college. The date was set and by the time the wedding would happen I would be eighteen years old, and it would be legal.

Colin, it turned out, was not so much of a racing car driver and much more of an 'in the pub every single night' kind of guy'. No wonder he worked behind the bar when I first met him, as he could get free alcohol all night, but I had no idea what alcoholism was at the time. Things started to deteriorate even further as the months went on and I wanted to cancel the wedding. I had seen behaviours in him that were deeply disturbing.

A horrendous cycle started of break-ups and make-ups that were endless. Something would happen, where I could not stand him any longer and I would try to leave but I never got very far as he would threaten to kill himself if I left. This was emotional blackmail, and I could see no way out, as every time he would fall apart, and fear would hit me like a bullet in the chest and I would change my mind again and stay so he did not die.

This backwards and forwards started to really take its toll on me, and I lost so much weight from the stress. I felt trapped by my fear, scared of what he may do to himself. Guilt washed over me every time I quietly tried to bring up the subject of not being sure this wedding was a good idea. I tried it from every angle, but it was useless. I was totally miserable and completely confused, powerless to end things cleanly once and for all. At one point I even ran away and stayed with my sister, who had just returned from being a nanny in Greece. She did not like what she had come home to and saw her little sister was in a terrible state. I told her everything and that I did not want to get married, and she agreed this had gone too far. We both tried to talk to our mother about it, but everything had been planned and paid for and it was way too late to stop it all. I felt terrible. She had even made my dress and would have been devastated if the whole thing had been cancelled. So, I went along with it, thinking I could run away afterwards and that is how I moved forward and stayed sane for just a bit longer. I sunk into a depressed state, and as his drinking escalated, I actually started to hate him, but felt completely trapped.

The dreaded wedding day finally arrived, and my mum had made me a dress with puffy sleeves and peach ribbons, kind of a Princess Diana knock-off. Whilst getting ready at my mum's house that morning, I begged her not to make me go ahead with the wedding. I begged, cried, locked myself in the bathroom, tried to reason with her but nothing was going to work. Even my sister tried to make her see sense, but she would not budge. It was way too late for that. This is the same thing that had happened with my mum marrying my father and it was way too late to lose face and back out at the last minute. History was repeating itself. People were on their way to the church, and I was going to have to go through with it.

Utterly miserable I walked down the aisle. I can honestly say I cannot remember anything at all. I knew this was the biggest mistake of my life and eventually I would get away. If this was love you could shove it; fairy tales did not mention this kind of shit going down!

A week after the wedding, Colin and I left for a holiday in Spain. I was dreading it. It turned out I did not have much to worry about. The drinks were included in the price and Colin had stocked up on duty free bottles of vodka, so from the moment we got there, he was locked in the room drinking his head off. I was just glad for the reprieve from his constant, suffocating neediness and suicide threats. You can only be threatened so many times before it stops having any effect on you. He was crying wolf and I was so dead inside, I honestly wished he would just do it, so I could be free from this nightmare.

I was very lucky on the holiday, as an elderly couple took me under their wing after they saw me alone at every mealtime and I told them what was happening. They were so lovely and let me spend time with them and then in the evenings I would creep back into my room trying not to wake Colin. As I walked in, the smell of alcohol made me feel sick. If I was lucky and went back really late, he would have passed out. It was much worse if he was still awake as he would be staggering around the room, making no sense at all, it was frightening.

We barely said a word to each other on the way home. I hated him with a vengeance by this time. He had basically lived his dream and spent the whole trip wasted and now had a massive hangover to contend with for the journey home. He puked in a bag the whole journey. It was disgusting but by now I was well and truly plotting my escape. There was no way I was staying. This time I was not scared at all. I was just done. Within a matter of days, I told him I was leaving for good this time, and nothing would stop me. Trouble was, I didn't have a car and had no way of leaving but I would walk if I had to as anything was better than being here.

I wandered around the countryside for a while and found a phone box and called my friend Theresa, who said she would come and get me with her older brother Bernard, and I could stay with their parents back in Gravesend for as long as I needed. Relieved, I went back to pack my things hoping they would be there soon. As I walked back into the property, I noticed my mother's car outside and knew exactly what had happened, because this was the pattern I had been living with now for so long. Colin had taken some pills and yet again called my mother, who raced to rescue him for about the sixth time; he had the game down well by now. The difference now was, I didn't give a shit any more.

As I walked in, Colin was being sick, vomiting up the pills he had taken. I ignored him and started to gather up my things. My mother was frantic and started trying to reason with me to stay and work things out, but she had no idea the extent of the abuse I was dealing with. I made it very clear I had hit the point of no return and was not coming back. I have no idea how I got out of there. He was freaking out, and my mother was telling me she would never speak to me again if I left. She was terrified he would die, and I would be responsible. She just wanted it all to be okay and I just felt so bad for her having to deal with this. I felt so guilty that I had brought this chaos to our family. I had wanted it all; the engagement and the wedding and now I wanted out and no one could understand because no one knew he was a drunk. It was all kept a secret and I was the wicked girl who had broken his heart. That is the story he wanted everyone to believe as he was such a victim. The big difference was he was an adult, and I had no idea what I was signing up for because I was just a child.

I spent the next year of my life living with Theresa's family who kindly took me in. Colin finally realized I was not coming back and tried to end his life again and this time he went to a psychiatric hospital where he was kept for a few months. When my mother convinced me I should visit him, I agreed to it as I wanted a divorce. When I arrived, a doctor took me to one side and explained that Colin would be there for a while longer as he was a very sick man and needed help. He also informed me that Colin had formed an attachment with another young girl on the ward who was being treated for anorexia and she had made a complaint that he had raped her. I was unshockable by this time as he had done the same thing to me when I had tried to leave previously. I informed the doctor that we were in the process of getting a divorce and any other information regarding Colin and his welfare needed to be told to his parents, as I would not be around. I then walked calmly into his room, where he lay in bed looking very sorry for himself. He smiled at me, hoping this was going to be the moment I would apologize for leaving and tell him we could get back together, but I had experienced a wake-up call and realized this was all a game and a manipulation that would no longer have any power over me. The bullshit had to stop. He was never going to actually kill himself; he just had the technique down to get attention and get me back to him. It worked every single time. He was so fucked up and damaged and was making me look like the crazy one for leaving his sorry ass.

I walked over to his bed and noticed he had just finished dinner. He looked pretty good actually, pretty pleased with himself and something inside me snapped. A large, clear jug of water came into my view and before I could even think about it, I had picked it up and thrown its contents straight in his face. The force of the water hit him so hard that his head shot back and then he just sat there soaking wet and for once he was the one looking scared. He had never seen me fight back. He had totally underestimated me from day one. As I left the room, I told him to do the job properly next time, or I would come and do it for him.

I walked away, out into the daylight and a huge sense of freedom came over me. I realised I had been the victim, not him. I had been emotionally blackmailed and abused by this person. It was now time to focus on me and stay away from men for a while as I clearly had no clue what the hell I was doing. Years later, Colin went on to marry again and had a child which did not surprise me at all; he could not stand to be alone. My mother stayed in touch with his family, and she let me know one day that he had passed away. She was very upset about it. He had a massive heart attack and died suddenly. I felt nothing, which surprised her as I am not a cold person, but on this subject, I was a cold-hearted bitch, and I was okay with that.

I had finally tapped into an inner strength that was always there deep down. I just didn't realize how strong I was until someone hit my limit.

I now think part of the problem is that I have never been with someone who is of 'equal magnitude'. I always settled for less, through fear of being alone and let my imagination bring people to life who were not really there at all. I just wanted to be 'normal' and in this perfect relationship so the outside world would know I was no longer the fuck-up and that I was finally getting my shit together. I was just as messed up at forty as I was at twenty, if not worse. My fucked-up history of relationships sent me to despair. I just could not get it right. What was wrong with me? Why did I keep getting it so very wrong?

So far, I have worked out this much. A person can spend their whole life running away from the past and they will keep repeating the same pattern until they look back and confront the monsters of the past and find peace with themselves, otherwise they will keep creating the same situation over and over. You have to make peace with yourself at some point. There are many things I would have done differently if I could. I know I have hurt people, good people who did not deserve it and I have been terribly hurt as well and that is just how life is at times in love. I have spent so many years trying everything available to fill the void that childhood trauma created in my life, and it did not work.

I mistakenly thought 'true love' was the butterflies you got when you first spotted someone you liked the look of, from across the room. It was a magical, mystical, elusive thing that could not be explained. I thought that somehow, somewhere out there was that one person for me, but I had just never met him. I believed somewhere on this planet, he was out there, and I just had to find him, or he had to find me. I had no idea how it even worked, but this is what I was doing. I was looking for love and the 'one' that we read about in fairy tales. I did find love of sorts now and then, but I never found a resting place and someone I felt safe with.

I guess that old saying of 'you have to learn to love yourself, before you can love anyone else', which made absolutely no sense to me at the time, was actually true. I have realised that now but previously the concept of loving myself was impossible, as I believed I was worthless, so how could that ever happen? It was ridiculous to even contemplate it.

I know now that our capacity to love ourselves is in direct proportion to our capacity to take responsibility and forgive ourselves. When we can take responsibility for our own acts against others, rather than pointing the finger at them, we then become pan-determined and can understand where another is coming from and why we might have deserved the treatment we were given. This is what leads to understanding and forgiveness. We are all human and loving each other has never been more important as it is today when the world is in such a mess.

I look back and I forgive Colin for the part he played, and I forgive myself for screwing up other really good relationships over the years. I was a slave to my unconscious patterns that I could not break.

The next years of my life were a roller coaster of long-term relationships that never worked out. After my escape from Colin, I had found my running shoes and the walls had come up and they were not going down again easily.

Time passed and eventually life took an unexpected turn as this ugly duckling started to blossom and I found myself discovered by a model agent in Norway whilst I was visiting friends and the next thing I knew; I was in front of three thousand people modelling swimwear at the Concert Hus in Oslo. No one was more shocked than me that anyone thought I was even remotely attractive. This was certainly not something I had expected. The shows were amazing, and I loved to travel, so it was the perfect fit. A few months later it was announced that our agency in Norway had been invited to Dallas to take part in something called The Face of the '80s. It was 1989 and I was thrilled to be included. The following week we arrived at a huge convention centre where agents from all over the country would come and sign new talent. I was amazed to be offered contracts with IMG in New York or Miami, with an agency called L'Agence, run by a husband-and-wife team. They felt like a safe choice, so I signed up and it was by the beach which sounded awesome, so I was on a plane within a few days.

In the European modelling world, Miami was the place to be from November to March, to shoot swimwear catalogues for the following summer and I got settled into the agency apartment with six other girls and started to work straight away. It was uncomfortable for me initially, to be sharing my space with these incredibly beautiful beings. They were stunning. I went from being the gawky, ugly kid to having my picture taken for a living and being told I was beautiful. I never believed it to be true and lived in total fear of being found out as the ugly duckling every day. I lived in fear that the agents would suddenly wake up and realise they had an ugly girl on the books and fire me.

One day, a gorgeous model moved in to the agency apartment who was a bit of a star, as she was the current Hawaiian Tropic Tanning Oil girl and did all their promotional material. She was there less than ten minutes, before she was bragging about the fact she was dating Donald Trump. Wow, I thought, lucky Donald. She moved in and out of the apartment so fast, we didn't have time to really get to know her as her boyfriend wanted her in New York and who could blame him.

It was such an exciting time, running around having my picture taken, getting hair and make-up done, being told I was gorgeous. It was all a bit too American for me at times, but I went along with it. My head started to expand for sure with all the compliments but to be honest, even when I saw the final images of myself, I still did not see what others did. There was a serious disconnect which I believe went back to my childhood. It had left me with a seriously underdeveloped sense of self-worth and self-image, so no matter what anyone told me, I did not believe them. I look back at these pictures now and see a beautiful, young woman on the outside who was filled with fear and self-loathing on the inside. No matter how good the pictures were, I did not feel pretty. It was beyond my capability. I was always comparing how others looked on the outside to how I felt on the inside, and I felt like an idiot for even being there. Time and again I kept hearing how you had to love yourself before you could love another and did not have a fucking clue what the hell that even meant! I had read literally every self-help book on the shelves of the bookstore by now and was still none the wiser.

My modelling career was pretty short-lived in Miami, as I stupidly had a very nasty fall from a polo pony a friend asked me to help her exercise. The horse was a youngster and straight off the track. He was being trained to become a high-goal pony and was fast as hell. Of course, I fell in love with him immediately and jumped on his back without hesitation, but it turned out he had not been ridden for a while and before I knew what was happening, he bucked at full speed and tossed me into the bushes, where I landed in a heap, having fractured the second vertebrae in my back and that was it: career over. I could not walk for a couple of months and when I could, it was time to go home to England, as I was now broke, and had medical bills piling up.

It was time to come home, back to a place I had been running from for years to lay my demons to rest and find peace and that is all I wanted to do. The fast lane had been interesting, but I was a fish out of water and needed to find a quieter, calmer life.

5

Gangsta's Paradise

Looking back at my early dating years it was obvious I was pretty damaged. It was fast dawning on me that when it came to love and romance, I was a hot mess and definitely had some issues I needed to handle. The guys I was attracted to seemed good on paper initially but clearly a little further down the line, once the 'honeymoon phase' was over, they showed their true colours by mainly lying or cheating and by then I had already drunk the Kool-Aid and had fallen down the rabbit hole.

To be honest, the fairy tale nonsense we are force fed as young girls has to be held accountable for most women being delusional when it comes to love. I knew I was not the only one having a nightmare love life, and reading stories such as *Cinderella*, *Beauty and The Beast* and *Sleeping Beauty* growing up had not helped the situation. These kinds of books actually set a girl up for complete failure. Add to that a dysfunctional childhood and no role modelling of a happy relationship and you really are lost at sea trying to navigate the stormy waters of love. No wonder the Bridget Jones movie was such a success, as we could all relate to sexual harassment in the workplace and dating complete idiots who just cheated on you over and over.

To be honest, I have to take some responsibility for encouraging the whole game as I used to get so swept up in the Mills and Boon love stories my mum used to leave lying around. There was always a handsome, mysterious, kind of Mark Darcy character who is difficult and mean to the young girl, who is in awe of him and after a few tricky situations it turns out he is a prince and wonderful, and they live happily ever after and all the problems dissolve. I mean Pleeeese, who really believes this crap? I guess I did and so did Bridget Jones. No wonder so much wine was necessary during the movie; it is how us girls go through our twenties and thirties with all this nonsense going on!

Meanwhile, back in London and alone again facing the future. I started to focus on finding a job that had nothing to do with the modelling world and let's face it, working as a model was not that well paid, unless you were Cindy Crawford and I was definitely not, plus it never made me feel secure so that gig was definitely over. The illusion that modelling is so glamorous was far from the reality of the situation as you were constantly being told all the reasons you were not right for a job, rather than how perfect you were for it. By the end of your career, you ended up with double the insecurities you started off with so I happily said goodbye to that world, and it was onwards and upwards for me and men could bugger off for now. Little did I know a new career was just around the corner.

To my surprise, after applying for a temporary contract at the investment bank Bear Stearns in Canary Wharf, I was offered a position as a personal assistant to the vice president of the derivatives desk and I discovered the trading floor to be an exciting, fast-paced environment, which was perfect for me. I started my SFA (trading exams) and then went on to the emerging markets desk at Salomon Smith Barney in Victoria. I was pretty happy with my life at this point. I lived alone and had good friends around me.

Most of this new crowd of friends were either models I had previously known or super-rich traders with a smattering of very glamorous, wealthy 'It Girls' on the London scene. It was never boring. I was never an 'It girl', in fact, I was the opposite of that, but I was surrounded by them including Kirsty Bertarelli, now the richest woman in England through marriage, Dana Malmstrom (daughter of the truly wonderful Mandy Rice Davies of the Profumo Scandal fame), Tara Palmer-Tomkinson and Jemima Goldsmith. God only knows how I ended up around this crowd of very wealthy, super beautiful, fun, smart girls but I did and to think I was just a little smart ass, street rat compared to them, but I was funny as hell so that paid my way in entertainment value. Most of the time I could not even begin to comprehend the wealth and privilege some of these girls had due to their parents buying them apartments, cars and a designer wardrobe. Sometimes I felt like I was the only one that actually had a job.

Funny how women look at the images in magazines and dream of looking like the models I was hanging out with. They were so beautiful and so thin and extremely popular with their amazing clothes, tanned, young skin, immaculate make-up and incredible freshly blow-dried hair. Of course, no one ever mentioned we were all on diet pills loaded with caffeine, which sent us all speeding from one party to another and add to that the laxatives and starvation we were all putting ourselves through. We were all practically dying trying to keep up this image and lifestyle. It was exhausting. It was hard to believe I managed to dodge the cocaine train, but I had very good reasons to not go down that road.

First off, I was a control freak and needed my wits about me at all times to feel safe due to the violence in my childhood. The hyper-vigilant state of mind never left me.

Secondly, I am deathly allergic to any kind of opiates and so is my mother, which is one of the annoying genetic traits I inherited, as this meant I could not even have good pain control after having wisdom teeth out. Trust me, the temptation has been there and now and then, I gave it a try, but it never worked for me. The last straw came after a girlfriend gave me a quarter of an ecstasy tablet in Tramp nightclub one night. She said it would keep me awake and I would feel great, so I washed it down with some champagne and then within ten minutes I was projectile vomiting in the bathroom — not exactly the desired effect, I am sure.

I soon found out street drugs and prescription drugs, such as opiates, were basically the same thing and fortunately, my friends relaxed the peer pressure and realised good drugs would be wasted on me and end up down the toilet within minutes, so I happily stuck to champagne or diet coke from then on and actually seemed to have much more fun than anyone else did.

The third reason for not getting into the drug scene was my cousin Ian died of a heroin overdose when he was in his twenties. He was the loveliest boy who got hooked on drugs in school as the dealers would wait outside the school gates and give the kids sweets at first and then speed to get them hooked. To think this still happens in our society is mind blowing. Ian struggled with addiction for many years and just did not have the right kind of help at his disposal. He was totally failed by the healthcare system in this country and whilst trying to come off this horrendous drug he lost his battle. So that was my reason to really be wary of the whole social drug scene, as I knew in the back of my mind, I did have an addictive personality and did not want to go down the path of no return. It scared me.

To be honest, once I realised a great deal of my friends and people I worked with were using, I stopped going out as I had started to get bored of the whole scene and things needed to change. The constant round of dinners, clubs, after-parties all sounds very exciting and it was for a while but let's face it, how many meaningful conversations could you really expect to have with a bunch of mainly blind drunk, drug addicts who may look fabulous but behind the facade they were just a mess.

Once I made the decision to be around healthier people, I started to spend my weekends differently and found it suited me. I was more alert, having not spent the night before drinking and I was up early and out in the morning working out and enjoying my day so much more without a hangover to contend with. The other added bonus to not going out was how much more productive at work I became. Instead of sitting there with a splitting headache, wishing the day was over, I actually became useful to the people around me and started to do really well. I also looked forward to my weekends more and avoided people who were calling me to go out and instead started to meet people who were on a different, more spiritual path. I truly believe in the power of manifestation because I soon met someone who would change my life in such a positive way, there was no way it was a coincidence.

I was staying with my girlfriend Dana in Knightsbridge and woke up early Saturday morning and put on my rollerblades and headed to Kensington Palace Gardens to skate and get a workout in. It was a sunny day and lots of people had the same idea as me and were out skating about and it was not long before I realized a cute guy was following me. As it turned out his name was Gary Cardone, and he was an American ex-patriot living in London. Now he was cute, but he was definitely not cool as he was wearing elbow pads that were a good idea if you were learning to skate, but not so smart if you wanted to attract the ladies!

Gary was a smalltown boy from Lake Charles, Louisiana and he had worked very hard to get to this point in his life. He was recently divorced and although he was not wealthy compared to the idiots I worked with, he was a grafter and had a huge passion and drive to make it big in Europe working for an American oil and gas trading company. After a few dates I found out a great deal more. His father had died when he was very young, and he had been raised by his mother. We connected over our childhood traumas and had a great deal of empathy for one another which is probably why we were attracted to each other on a deeper level. We were both survivors for sure. He also had a twin brother called Grant who was successful in America as a motivational speaker in the automotive industry. I got the impression there was some healthy competition between them.

Gary was very serious about work and had an intensity about him that was unnerving at times. The best thing about him was that he was absolutely not into any kind of party lifestyle; he did not drink or do drugs and he was a spiritual man on a quest to find the answers to the bigger picture of life and livingness. He was nothing like anyone I had ever met before and that was such a refreshing change. I had finally met a person I could hold a meaningful conversation with and believed he had some of the answers I might have been looking for to life, living and spirituality. There was only one problem with the whole picture: he was newly divorced and was not looking for a relationship or love. He was looking for fun and that was at odds with what I wanted. Not that I wanted to get married again; seriously, I had been there and done that, but I was not the 'fun girl'. I was a commitment girl who fell in love too quickly and wanted to find my resting place and build something lasting. I was just not into a casual situation, never have been and maybe that is where the problem was for me, as I cannot be intimate with someone I do not love.

Regardless of wanting different things in a relationship, Gary and I dated on and off, not really quite ever getting ourselves together to have a serious relationship. We limped along and sadly by the middle of 1996 we broke up and went our separate ways. He was very honest about it; he was not in love with me, and I had already told him I loved him on a recent holiday to the Caribbean, so it was time for me to face the truth and walk away. I was gutted but knew it was not working out for either of us and so my 'It Girl' friends rallied around me, and I hit Tramps and Annabelle's once again, trying to just move on and get him out of my mind.

It was on one of these nights at Tramps that my friend Robert Tchenguiz said he wanted to introduce me to a friend of his and as I looked behind, there stood the tall dark-haired man who was listening to everything we were saying, and I was just not in the mood to be fixed up with anyone. It was a Thursday night, it was late, and I was tired, plus I had work in the morning and just wanted to go home. The friend heard me say I was leaving and had a kind of sad puppy dog expression on his face, and I felt bad for him and hated being mean to anyone, so I agreed to say a quick hello.

His name was Dodi al Fayed and as I got closer, I noticed how kind and sober he looked which was rare in Tramps. I told him I could stay for just a little longer and he seemed happy with that. We sat down and drinks were brought to our table and as I sipped on my champagne 'Gangsta's Paradise' by Coolio came on and he asked me to dance, and as we left the table, I got the first clue as to who he was because he placed a white napkin over his glass to protect it which struck me as odd, but I ignored it. I had no idea at the time this was something he did for his own safety, as he had been raised in a world where people got drugged and kidnapped if they were not careful.

The dance floor was packed as usual, and I found a space in front of the DJ, and something happened that I did not expect: the guy could actually dance. I was pretty shocked, and he laughed at my surprise, took my hands and looked right into my eyes, no shyness at all. He just had a big, beautiful smile and he melted me, and as the song finished, a slow one came on next, so we stayed right where we were, and he took me in his arms, and we just clicked and laughed as we both realised this felt good and just kind of worked. Clearly, he was comfortable in this scene and was not a stranger to beautiful women; in fact, I found out later, after dating him for a while, I looked just like his ex-wife, Suzanne, we had both been models and had identical long, curly, blonde hair and similar facial features. It must have been that reason why he singled me out. I was just his type.

By the time we made it back to the table, the glass with the napkin on it had gone and as we sat down it was immediately replaced with another fresh drink by Guido the Maître d'. He certainly had the staff well trained here I remember thinking. It was now time for me to go home and he immediately stood up, like the perfect gentleman he was and asked me if he could give me a lift home or call me and take me to dinner next week. I declined the ride home, preferring to take a taxi and gave him my phone number. After all, first dances like that did not come along every day and after my last heartbreak I was ready to laugh again for sure.

Over the next few months, we started to see quite a bit of each other, and our routine followed the same pattern most of the time. I would meet him at his apartment on Park Lane, where we would have a glass of champagne in the sitting room. His apartment was on two floors with everything decorated in neutral colours, with white sofas. It was very light and airy. He had family pictures all around the sitting area and the kitchen was open plan and spotless. It looked like no one ever cooked in it. The master bedroom was downstairs and as you walked down; you passed a wall of uniforms on display behind glass. One of them was pure white and from Sandhurst apparently. It was all very *Officer and a Gentleman,* and I am sure it went down very well with the ladies! I was starting to realise he was the quintessential playboy, albeit a very shy one.

Dodi had some quirks about him that I never fully understood until much later on. By now I knew his father owned Harrods and that Dodi had been married before and was currently single. If Dodi was seeing anyone else at the time, it was not something I could easily find out about and was not a subject we discussed. Dodi travelled a great deal and was often in LA or Paris and I would have been stupid to think he never went out with anyone else, but I also knew what we had was not just casual. I felt it when we were alone together, and when we looked at each other. He was protective and a little jealous if anyone else talked to me when we went out. I liked that he did not drink very much and would never let me drink and drive. He had a serious issue with that and made sure I was always picked up or taken home or I had the guest room to sleep in before we started sharing the same bed.

Dodi was actually very shrewd and frugal; he did not do the vulgar displays of wealth that I had become used to. The only thing that used to bug me was the number of stupid people who tagged along when we went out. Of course, I was polite to his entourage, but I was definitely not on friendly terms with any of them, especially when we all went back to Dodi's apartment for drinks, at the end of the evening. The hangers-on were sketchy guys, albeit in smart suits, wearing strong cologne. I was not the only one uncomfortable as Dodi himself was clearly ill at ease most of the time around this crowd. I did not understand why they were always lurking in the background, listening to every conversation, their status at the table obvious due to their lack of ever picking up a tab for dinner or a drink. It felt like they either worked for him or were 'old' friends who could hold a conversation in a group because that was not his thing. He was not a raconteur and preferred to stay quiet around other people. In fact, he was almost paranoid about talking in public or verbalising his own opinion. He was very passive and withdrawn at times; it was as though he felt he was being watched constantly or listened to.

I did not understand why this lovely man was so anxious; it was confusing. He was not confident personally and considering his career was in the movie industry as a producer raising finance for films such as *Chariots of Fire* and *The Scarlet Letter*, you would think he would be very dynamic, but he was quiet, subtle and guarded most of the time.

We were still dating as Christmas loomed ahead of us and Dodi asked me to go to Colorado with him as he had been invited by his friends Bruce Willis and Demi Moore who owned a home there. I told Dodi that I would see how much time I could get off work. We started to make tentative plans and I got really excited as this would be our first trip together, but I was also playing it cool, not wanting to seem too eager. He asked me what I wanted for Christmas and as I was planning to study for a degree in psychology at The University of Richmond, I told him I wanted some books on the subject and he thought that was a great idea.

A few weeks before Christmas, Dodi told me he would be away on business, but he would sort the trip out and be in touch with the details and I just left it at that. Christmas came and went, and I heard nothing from him. I had never been the girl that blows up a guy's phone and so I just went into silent mode and did nothing. When it became obvious it was over, I was disappointed for sure, but it was not the end of the world, just the end of our situation and to be honest I pretty much had enough of the constant disappointment from men by then. I really knew I deserved much more and brushed it off because in all fairness I was still rebounding from Gary, who was in my thoughts most of the time and who had started to reach out here and there as he felt he may have made a mistake in breaking up with me.

So there started a complicated triangle with the three of us, as I tried to figure out what to do with two men who seemed interested in me, but clearly were sending mixed signals and playing a game called reach and withdraw emotionally. They could not just let me be. It was so confusing.

Of course with all this going on it was inevitable that our time together would come to an end. The final straw happened at a party when I saw him disappear into another room with someone and I knew it was over. I felt disrespected and pissed off, so I grabbed my bag and went out to his driver and asked him to take me home. He refused and said it would cost him his job, but I managed to convince him that Dodi would not even notice I was gone and by then the car would be back and he would be none the wiser and it worked because I got my ride home.

Later that night my phone kept ringing and I knew it was Dodi and it was way too late for any more excuses. He was just not that into me and I got it. I was never the dumb girl and pretty much knew when to walk away. At least I had that going for me.

Endings are never easy but for some reason this one was particularly hard. I doubt there were many occasions when Dodi did not get his way when it came to women, and I had the feeling it was only when he lost something that he realised its true value. The truth was I still had feelings for Gary and whilst Dodi was fun, we were both just lonely. I cared for him but neither of us was in love by any means and I did not want to settle for anything less.

There were so many other reasons this would never work as I could not do the nightclubs and parties any more; it was exhausting, and I was always tired at work the next day, as our evenings always ran so late, and it was always on his schedule rather than mine. So, when he asked me to meet him at his apartment so he could explain what happened at the party, I agreed and knew this was going to be closure for me on a chapter of my life. I knew it was time to stop hurting myself and this time make the change of scene permanent as it was always so tempting to drift back to the party rather than sit home alone. It was time to grow up and walk away.

As I knew he would, Dodi had a million reasons as to why he was with the other girl at the party, but I just did not care any more. He said he had made a mistake and asked me again for another chance, but I was not budging. He even dropped to his knees and pleaded with me, telling me he loved me. I will never forget the sound of Dodi crying and begging me to stay and to give him another chance, but it was just too late. I needed to say goodbye and exit the apartment before I changed my mind, which was totally possible. By now I knew enough about Dodi to know that he did not respond well to the word no and he was always the one to leave so being abandoned (as he viewed it) was really distressing to him so I really was willing to try again as I knew how painful being left is. So I decided to test the love he professed and how he answered the questions would show me how he really felt deep down. I was tired of wondering if he loved me because I looked so much like his ex-wife Suzanne. The thought had crossed my mind more than once.

I found myself telling Dodi that I would ask him three questions and if he got one right, I would stay and work it out. It was like a proof of love test to see if we were right for each other. He looked hopeful and stood up. This would turn into a defining moment in my life, where I found a way to respect myself enough to leave someone who did not love me enough. I knew in my heart he really cared, but just not enough and I just wanted to get off the emotional roller coaster I found myself chained to through low self-esteem and loneliness. I just was not going to settle for anything less than someone 'in love' with me. Someone who would go above and beyond to show me, rather than just tell me he loved me. So, I asked Dodi the following simple questions as a way for him to back up what he had just said.

The first question was: What is my phone number? So, Dodi did not have an answer to this. Why? Because his secretary would call me. He usually would not pick up the phone until I was on the line. In my viewpoint if you truly care and are madly and deeply in love with someone you would pick up the damn phone yourself and call that person every chance you had and because you had phoned them so often, you would know their number.

Second question: What is my address? Now I am not expecting an exact street number; a general location would have been acceptable, but yet again Dodi did not have an answer. He looked a little confused and obviously was wondering why a successful, intelligent man, who had a driver at his disposal 24/7 would have to know something like that. The point is this. He did not know my address because I always drove to his place, or he sent his bloody driver. He was not even in the damn car when it arrived. I was picked up and then I was taken back to his apartment to pick him up. Seriously? He went to Sandhurst for God's sake. Had he not watched Richard Gere sweep the girl off her feet in *An Officer and a Gentleman*? Obviously not.

Third question: What had I asked him to get me for Christmas? Dodi perked up as he knew the answer and quickly told me books! He was pretty proud of himself, bless him and smiled at me as he thought he had nailed the last question, but I had one more.

Last question: Dodi, what did you actually get me for Christmas? And there it was, the truth laid out in front of us. There was a silence as he processed what had just happened. The answer was he got me nothing. It did not even need to be said and he knew it. I quietly and gently explained to him this was not love. You did not treat a woman you loved this way and he just stood there looking back at me. I felt like a total bitch but knew I had to leave. Looking back, I honestly think he just hated anyone leaving him. I knew by now his childhood issues of abandonment triggered panic in him and when someone threatened to leave him, he could not take it and would revert to being a child begging that person not to leave.

As I left the apartment, he was calling out for me to wait but I did not look back. I shut the door behind me and walked down the long winding staircase, not wanting to get into the elevator as it would have taken too long. I needed to feel the fresh air and feel like I could breathe again. Something had changed in me, and I had stopped thinking everyone else was more important than I was. I had finally been able to hold my head up and know I was worth so much more. It was a defining moment and one I will never forget. I had finally changed and was starting to learn to love myself for the first time in my life.

For the next few months, I just kept my head down and honestly felt like I had given up on love, especially in London where pretty girls were ten a penny and good looking, wealthy guys could call the shots and keep their options open at all times, so it was very surprising to me that Gary reached out again and said he missed me and that this time he wanted to work things out and sounded serious about it. Something had changed for sure, so we met for dinner, and both realised how much we had missed each other. Finally, things were falling into place and having spent the last year and a half trying to get him to love me, he finally seemed to accept that he did.

Things moved very quickly for us after that dinner and Gary suggested we live together as a sign of his commitment and even wanted to buy a house in Richmond, as he was obviously staying for longer than just a few years and I was really happy to hear that. We started the house hunt and by July we found a beautiful place called 'The Crow's Nest' and got it for a great deal. The day we moved in the wisteria was out in the garden, wrapping itself around the house, its lilac blossoms saying welcome home. It was now officially my favourite time of year. I just could not believe for the first time in my life I felt safe, happy and loved.

Maybe a prince does come along now and then and there can be a happy ever after for little street rats like me. Maybe it is not just the 'It Girls' that get the guy and swan off into the sunset to live their perfect lives. If a messed-up girl, who came from nothing, can have her dream come true then anyone can.

I was not the only one who found happiness that summer as Dodi seemed to move on pretty fast too and the last time we spoke, he told me he had met someone very special, and I was happy for him. He was making big plans and was clearly in love in a way that I had never seen. Of course, it was not long before the tabloids' headlines started screaming out the news that Dodi was now dating Princess Diana, he had found the person he was looking for, finally, and all those other girls, including me, who were clearly never right could see how different he was with her. He was a man in love and had no problem with the world knowing as he was proud to be in this relationship with someone who finally was there for the right reasons, not what they could get from him and then, as if just to prove the point, up popped Kelly Fisher in the tabloids and then on the television working every angle she could think of with her lawyer in tow leading her down a very silly path with her accusations of breach of promise and ridiculous legal action.

I remember watching Kelly give an interview at the time and thought to myself, good God, woman, pull yourself together, this is not doing you any favours at all! She alleged they were engaged and wore an identical ring to the one given to Princess Diana by Prince Charles. This was just getting ridiculous — talk about milking a moment. I actually did not believe her at all and knew she was just looking for some kind of financial compensation, as it all just sounded absurd and felt like the circus had come to town and I wanted no part of it, so I kept my head down and my mouth shut. Dodi was doing the same, or at least trying to but the media was not going away. Why would they as they were doing what they had always done, providing the people with what they wanted.

Gary and I had discussed my relationship with Dodi before we got back together and had openly discussed this with trusted friends during a dinner party once the story started to break. The real reason I called it a day with Dodi was talked about and it is not something I would have wanted made public. We were therefore pretty shocked to find out the story had come to the attention of the media and this left us no choice but to seek legal advice and take action to shut it down. We quickly saw a solicitor in London who served a cease and desist document to the relevant parties.

We were lucky our friend, Paul Hawkes, a renowned Private Investigator and Principal of Research Associates, had stepped in to help navigate this difficult time. It was because of his action this story never made it to the light of day.

The last thing we wanted was my name dragged into this big mess, especially as I was seeing Dodi being torn to shreds in the media and I was not going to add more fuel to the fire as this man had done nothing to harm me and did not deserve what he was being subjected to for loving Diana.

Dodi was handling things the best way he knew how and had been brave enough to send a big message to the world with the images from the Jonikal of them kissing. He hoped the images would be enough for them to get some space, but he underestimated the public's desire for more and even though the people were happy to see Diana moving on they just could not get enough of this new story.

To many this romance was very exciting news as it is not every day a princess falls in love with a playboy, instead of a prince. The world was curious to know if this was love. Has Dodi finally found the one? Was he ready to settle down? Of course, the answer is yes, he was, he had made that very clear to me in our last conversation. He had been ready to settle down for a long time and have a family and had been looking for the right woman for a while now. He was ready for love and to be loved, in fact he absolutely craved it. I cannot speak for Diana as I never knew her and only met her once briefly, at a dinner in London at the Portuguese Embassy the year before, but my goodness, she was charismatic and stunning in person, so how could he not be madly in love? They were a great match in my own opinion.

The press continued to go crazy for any information they could get about Dodi as he was relatively unknown to the general public. Old so-called friends of his started popping up and they were not very helpful but then most of them never had been. Any man Diana would have been interested in was sure to come under a huge amount of scrutiny and in most cases this would not be welcome. The kind of men she dated previously were publicity shy and not keen on being dragged through the mill, except maybe James Hewitt, who seemed to enjoy his five minutes if the price was right. The circus raged on through Saint Tropez and then to Paris where I noticed they seemed to be sending a message to the world.

Some dates will always be remembered in time due to some earth-shattering event that takes place that makes us all stop in our tracks. JFK being shot is one of them. Martin Luther King being assassinated is absolutely another. For many, Sunday 31st August 1997 was one the most poignant in history, because the world lost a princess who was loved by millions of people and had touched the hearts of us all.

I was asleep when the phone rang early in the morning and Gary answered the call. My friend Jo was on the line, and she told us to turn on the news as Dodi al Fayed had been killed in a car accident in Paris. We turned on the TV and there was no other news at that time, except the certainty that Dodi had died, and Diana was in hospital. Gary went to make coffee and I just sat and stared at the screen. It was not very long before it was announced that Princess Diana had also died, and the world went into mourning.

I know one thing for sure: Princess Diana died knowing what it was like to have a man who was in love with her. I believe this was the real deal for Dodi and I am sure he could see marriage and children in their future. He was in love and was a relationship guy and a family man so that would have been the next natural step for him. The night they died he was doing everything in his power to protect the woman he loved. You really cannot say more than that.

Looking back, it was not even the press that could be blamed for their death as they were just feeding the insatiable appetite of the public who wanted to know everything about this woman. That is what sold newspapers and we are all guilty of buying into the narrative in some way. I know it would have given Dodi huge anxiety to be so visible, but he would have done that for love and no other reason. As for Diana I am one hundred percent sure that she died knowing what it was like to be loved by a kind man. Dodi was affectionate, tactile, loving and pretty great in the bedroom and I for one am glad she experienced that side of him. I doubt she had felt that in many of her relationships. There was a tenderness to Dodi, it was as though he gave his soul to you in the bedroom as well as his heart. He was just so loving and special. Over the years when friends have asked me what Dodi was like I would always smile and say Diana died happy and although that sounds odd I believe it.

About six months after the accident, I was in Harrods, and I saw his father Mohammed Al Fayed walking through the store with his security. I really wanted to pay my respects and I asked his security if that would be possible and they said he would not want to be disturbed, he was grieving which I perfectly understood. I just watched as he went past and sent him love and light and hoped he would one day find peace. As time went by, it irritated me that not many people came to Dodi's defence in the aftermath.

Where were all those so-called friends who had surrounded us when we were dating?

On 7th April 2008, the jury verdict was that Diana and Dodi had been unlawfully killed, through the gross negligence of the chauffeur Henri Paul who was intoxicated. This fact was disputed by Mohammed Al Fayed and the driver's parents. When the driver's autopsy was made public information, I was curious and found it very disturbing as it seemed there was another culprit involved in this accident.

Henri Paul, since June 1996, had been prescribed Prozac (also known as Fluoxetine) and Tiapride to treat aggressiveness in alcoholics. Having lived in Paris myself, I know that it is more expensive to buy vitamins than it is to get psychiatric drugs and so it was common that people were on them. They seem to be everywhere. It is a shame that the most beautiful city in the world is also one of the most suppressed but I guess a population suppressed on medication is much more controllable and so it was not difficult to start to see the bigger picture.

The pharmaceutical drugs in Henri Paul's bloodstream were lethal, especially when mixed with alcohol or each other. The side effects of Prozac (fluoxetine) alone are nausea, vomiting, diarrhoea, sexual dysfunction, agitation, nervousness, restlessness, tremor and the most dangerous side effect is an overstimulation reaction and has been linked to thoughts of suicide and violence.

Tiapride was also found in the autopsy and is prescribed for the treatment of aggressiveness in alcoholics. The side effects of this drug include increased agitation, reduced concentration and impaired vision when mixed with alcohol. "Prudence of these drugs is generally recommended for drivers of vehicles," stated the French prosecutors' office in France.

Psychiatry had played a significant part in the loss of life and as the world went into a total meltdown over Diana, Dodi ended up looking like the villain who hired someone who was intoxicated when in fact he had no idea the man had even been drinking.

One of the last photographs released of the couple was from video footage of Diana and Dodi as they came down the elevator at the Ritz. Dodi had his head on her shoulder and his arms wrapped around her, clearly a man in love. It is hard to believe that was twenty-five years ago. Even today, Princess Diana is in the news constantly. Thankfully there have been so many positive things that have come from this event, especially when you see her sons go public about their own mental health struggles after her death. I would have really liked to see Henri Paul's psychiatrist take some responsibility for this accident, but of course that will never happen. The main focus was on the alcohol content in this blood and the prescription pills were not given enough news time for sure.

As for Dodi al Fayed, he was a really kind and decent human being who deserved better treatment than he got from his so-called friends of the time. He gave me a gift without even knowing it and that was the gift of loving myself enough to say goodbye to him. It was a defining moment in my life that I knew would always stay with me. I had never felt prouder of myself, as when I walked out of his apartment with my head held high, knowing this was not the path I wanted to take and that I was not willing to play that game any longer. True, my days would have been numbered anyway with Diana in the picture but I did not wait for that to happen. I made a decision that I deserved more, and I stuck to my guns.

At the end of the day, I loved Dodi, and was very upset when he died, our time together was beautiful and although we were not each other's resting place, we had shared something special, and I was proud to have known such a decent person who would have done anything for anyone and all he wanted in return was for people to love him back and not want him for anything more. I like to believe Diana gave him that and feel they would have been extremely happy together as both shy, damaged, kindred spirits finding a resting place with each other. There is not a shadow of doubt in my mind that he would have proposed to Diana and, having been on the receiving end of his love and attention, I know he would have made her feel loved, wanted and cherished, because that is who he was. In so many ways their coming together was a perfect union but sadly we never had the chance to see it play out.

These days when I hear Gangsta's Paradise I am transported back to the night we met and the kind man who looked deep into my soul, who was so sweet and full of hope to find love.

Gary and I got married a few years later and my fairy tale ending had some more twists and turns for sure but during this time there were some key moments that would help me later on when I went through hell during menopause.

6

Arizona Skies

The water from the shower hit me hard and as I stood shaking from head to toe, I knew I was in deep trouble. What had transpired in the last few days was more than I could take. Events of the previous week had traumatised me more than I had let on even to myself. Two years had passed since the Dodi and Diana tragedy and Gary, and I were busy getting on with our lives and were very happy. We married in January 1999 at Richmond registry office and then had fourteen friends for lunch at Cliveden Hotel in the stunning French Dining Room. We had also started IVF and were both more than ready and very excited to start a family. I really wanted to have a child with the man I loved, who was my resting place, of that I was certain.

Anyone who has been through IVF will testify that this is not for the faint of heart and could take its toll on both parties, but we thought we were up for the challenge and unbreakable. Gary always had extremely high standards of himself and others. He worked hard and worked out even harder. He was incredibly good-looking, the best-looking man I had ever dated. Sometimes I would just stare at him whilst he got ready for work and wonder how I got so damn lucky. It was not just the looks; he was smart, sexy, super fun and spontaneous. Even more than any of that I trusted someone, completely, for the first time in my life. I felt at peace and protected. To others looking in, I am sure I looked like the trophy wife of some rich dude but honestly, that was not the case at all. Gary had a good job, but he was not wealthy at that point. He often felt like the poor kid in comparison to all his super wealthy friends, and wanted to be up with the big boys, and my job was to make sure he was happy so he could reach his full potential. It was not even about money for him; it was about security and to be able to help others. I was so proud to be his wife, Mrs Annie Cardone, but I was even more humbled to be in his presence as he was my role model, mentor and guide and showed me a life that I had never had before. One that was safe and that had nothing to do with money.

Gary was a driven individual right from the get-go, with a twin brother, who was very successful on the motivational speaking circuit in America. He was determined to do as well in his field, and he did, as he was the president of Dynegy Europe by the end of our marriage. He worked his way through the ranks and proved himself over and over to be a Rottweiler at oil and gas trading and was untouchable. He was so savvy, but like me, he also had an unnerving intuition that left people stunned.

I was in nesting mode, decorating my dream house and making cute baby plans for our family that was most surely on its way with our first IVF attempt. The longer-term plan was to flip the house and get something further out in the countryside one day.

Life was amazing, my husband was incredible, we had a beautiful home, great friends, my family loved him, and we had our lives ahead of us. I had spent years watching my friends raise their children and had created bedrooms for them in my home, decorated just for them. I had an old rocking horse in the corner and pompoms on the curtains which looked so cute in the playroom. My goddaughter, Matilda, still calls me Pompom. She is now a teenager and still has that rocking horse. I have no idea where the time went some days. Nothing made me happier than to have my best friend's children stay over and put smiles on their faces. I knew motherhood was something I was more than ready for.

IVF is a monster of a treatment and not for the faint of heart. As I look back now knowing what I now know about hormones, I am amazed I came through it. If you ever have experienced PMS, times that by about ten thousand and you are getting an idea of what your body goes through. Being injected daily and pumped full of hormones, to trick your body into thinking it's pregnant and to make lots of eggs fertilise and create a baby is the biggest emotional and mental roller coaster you can go through. I had no idea of the devastating effect it would have on the delicate balance of my endocrine system. Would have been great if my doctors had given me a heads-up that I may turn into a raving lunatic who could not sleep, eat or function but no, they didn't have a clue. It is totally shocking to me now that when IVF fails to get you pregnant, the hormone injections stop point blank and you are left to your own devices as your progesterone and oestrogen plummets back down to earth turning on a mini menopause that itself that can lead to panic attacks, insomnia and depression. Not only do you have the hormones to worry about, but you also have failed to make a baby and that is the worst feeling in the world. The loss of my dream of having a child of my own with the man I loved was devastating.

I do hope things have changed for women since I did my last attempt and that they are left better equipped for what they will experience emotionally, physically and mentally. There must be a way to slowly come down from the injections rather than leaving you to fend for yourself. By now I was in my late thirties, and it was definitely now or never to have a family. I had no idea that just a short time later, instead of holding a baby in my arms, I would be locked up in a treatment centre in Phoenix, Arizona and staring down the barrel at the end of my marriage, suffering from panic attacks and severe depression. How anything could go that wrong that fast was beyond belief and it was all down to my endocrine system crashing hard.

Sadly, for Gary and I, our attempt at IVF was not meant to be successful and the doctors told me to take a break and maybe we could try again. Gary had other ideas and wanted to wait. To be honest, he had not been as excited as I was through the whole process but was supporting the idea on the surface of things. We tried again and this time when the eggs were harvested and Gary gave his sample, things took a very bad turn. None of the eggs had fertilised. I did not really receive much of an explanation from the doctors; they just told me it happens sometimes, and I went home totally devastated. I went totally downhill from there, and as the hormone drugs had been stopped completely, I was now a complete wreck.

Gone was my last chance of having a family. I was on a roller coaster of emotions from this news and on top of that my hormones were completely whacked out. As my thoughts started racing and sleep eluded me, the panic attacks started to kick in and I felt out of control and helpless as I tried to hide it from my husband. I could not bring myself to have a conversation with him about it and was silently imploding.

My emotions and reactions to this whole situation were not under my control mainly due to the depletion of vital hormones my body and brain needed to function. I felt like I was literally dying and breaking into pieces and if this sounds dramatic then it is because it was. Everything is magnified when hormones disappear. For me it all came back to proof of love and actions speaking louder than words. Had I missed something? Why did Gary not want to keep trying? Was this man not actually in love with me, because from where I was standing, the message was loud and clear. I was not his resting place at all, and he did not want to try and have a family with me again anytime soon. There was another element as to why the IVF had failed but Gary and I have laid that ghost to rest many years ago and some things do have to remain private.

Gary was blindsided at how unstable I was emotionally and did not want to subject me to any more pain. He could see I was totally spinning and could not slow down. The more I pushed the thoughts down, the more powerful they got, and it was not long before the world came crashing down around me.

I could barely breathe as the panic welled up inside me, but I managed to get up off the shower floor, get dressed and get out of the house. I drove towards central London, and on the way, I received a phone call from a friend asking me if I wanted to meet for lunch and it sounded like a good distraction. As I walked into the restaurant, she was sitting there smiling and next to her, at the table was an ex-boyfriend of mine. I had totally been set up. I should have left but the thought of going home to a deafening house and climbing the walls did not seem like a good plan, so I made the fatal mistake of staying.

Lunch, of course, came with drinks and to be honest, I was not feeling great physically. I wanted to leave, as I felt like I was speeding up even more. The effect of the alcohol was not helping, and I started to open up about what was happening in my life. After lunch I got in the car and started to feel very ill. My head was throbbing, and my thoughts started racing. I honestly thought I was having a nervous breakdown. Intending to drop my friends off on the way out of London I decided instead to have coffee with them and just get myself together.

When I eventually made it home, I knew I was in major trouble and needed help. I got in the shower and my mind was racing. As I slid down the wet glass walls and lay on the floor, I knew I was having a breakdown and there was nothing I could do to stop it. It was only years later in a therapy session that I had the cognition that my drinks had been spiked during lunch. Having been subjected to the same thing years ago as a model in Miami and I realised my bad reaction to the drugs were identical each time. This is one of the benefits of being allergic to opiates, you tend to get really ill and have to be very careful what you take. Sadly, I did not catch on to this in the moment and just thought I was losing my mind. I ended up telling Gary what was happening and that I was terrified and out of control and things happened very quickly after that and before I knew it, I was on a flight to a treatment centre for depression in Arizona. Gary had found me a safe place to go, and I had never been more relieved.

Arriving in Phoenix I was put in a wheelchair and taken off the flight. Almost unconscious, talk about a dramatic arrival. A so-called friend had come with me and given me a massive dosage of pain medication to help me sleep and she had nearly killed me. I was not used to taking medication of any kind and was allergic to opiates, so whatever she gave me had a terrible effect. I managed to wake up a few times, briefly, but could not speak and could only make sounds instead of words, it was terrifying. On landing, we were supposed to be met by a car from the facility, but it was not there and somehow, I woke up and found myself sprawled out in the back of a massive limo and then I would pass out again within seconds.

I have no idea how long we were in the car driving to the treatment centre, but I remember the car stopping and being woken up and told we had to get out of the car. I tried my best to come to but just could not make it, so as the inpatients sat in the serenity garden at the front entrance of The Meadows, doing their afternoon guided meditation, they were rudely interrupted by the sight of me literally falling out of the limo. A sense of excitement coursed around the group; they were hoping a massive celebrity like Madonna was checking in, as this is literally where the rich and famous detoxed, but they were soon disappointed when I landed on the ground resembling roadkill. I am sure I was a warning to everyone in the serenity garden that day, not to drink and do drugs. I probably helped them all in that moment as a reminder of what hell looks like as I am sure they just thought I was shit-faced instead of dealing with a massive hormone crash and raging insomnia. IVF failure is hard enough, but nothing prepares you for the rapid depletion of hormones. I had no idea myself until years later as I hit perimenopause and I was subjected to the exact same breakdown and symptoms and that is when it all started to fall into place.

Back at The Meadows, still flat out on the tarmac, a couple of nurses appeared and I assume they scraped me off the floor and took me inside for the invasive check-in process, aka 'search for drugs'. The nurses wanted to communicate with me, but I still could not speak. I was in a horror movie I could not wake up from and just wanted to sleep or die; either would do as anything was better than this. I could understand what they were saying but I could not speak and if I could have communicated, I still would have no clue as to the medication I had been given, so would not have been any help anyway.

The Meadows, it turned out, was not just a centre for the treatment of depression, it is also very well known as an addiction clinic, treating extremely wealthy people, hooked on sex, drugs and rock and roll. The only reason I ended up there was because most of Gary's uber wealthy 'friends' had spent time there. In fact, from what I could gather, it was like a second home for most of them by now, as they were in and out so often. It was almost like a private members club, it was so exclusive. When I eventually woke up in my room the next day, I saw a funny card next to my bed. It was from the woman who had flown with me. She wished me well and apologised for almost polishing me off on the plane with her pills. I felt bad for her having flown all that way to have to turn around and fly all the way back, but I could not have done it on my own, so I was grateful even though I was judged pretty harshly by others for trying to get her an upgrade on the flight, as I felt so bad for her having to travel all that way and head straight back. I was even told by some they doubted I had reached rock bottom. You sure find out who your friends are at times like this and those that use a moment of suffering to judge and condemn you.

Back in The Meadows I was pretty much given a tour and assigned a therapist and introduced to my psychiatrist, the very weird-looking Dr Wolf. He actually had very wild grey hair and a beard; the name most certainly did fit the bill. I was evaluated and put into a group of people who were sharing their stories. Still not quite in full charge of my speech faculties, I kept quiet and just observed. Later that day I was allowed a phone call to my husband to check in. It was brief and he asked how I was, but things were still very fuzzy and as I stood in the hallway, I noticed a new intake in the nurses' station. I heard her voice before I actually saw her, and she was most definitely British. Things were looking up; at least now I may have a British buddy to help me through this. As she turned around, I realised it was London's ultimate 'It Girl', the very beautiful and fabulous Tara Palmer-Tomkinson. Holy shit, I thought, this really was the place to be, thank God, I had a friend on the inside!

Over the next few days, Tara and I met up and, of course, we had been in the same circles and knew a lot of the same people. For me this was a definite improvement; at least I knew I was not going to be bored. We quickly became inseparable and had every breakfast, lunch and dinner together. We sat by the pool, played ping pong (she was bloody good at it) and laughed about our stories of life and the crazy social scene in London. She had the inside scoop on Prince Charles and Camilla, as she was his goddaughter and she told me they were very happy and perfect for each other as she was funny and outgoing and didn't take any shit from the future King of England. Tara and her family loved seeing them happy at last. Although Charles got so much public abuse for the way things played out, to be fair he had no choice in the matter. The pressure he was under to marry was not something he could shrug off. He thought he was doing the right thing by letting Camilla go and trying to make things work with Diana but it was just not meant to be and in the end they both transgressed in their marriage which was doomed from the start. I like to think that things would have gone very differently if Paris had not happened and both Charles and Diana would have found their happy ever after with people they were destined for but maybe that is just my soppy, romantic view of love.

Back at the Meadows Tara and I soon got into a routine, and it was fast becoming home. In situations like these, people bond very quickly and have a survivor mentality going on. I was not sure we would have been best friends out there in the real world, as we came from very different backgrounds and I had left that social circle of people she was around, a long time ago. But in this place and under the circumstances of our lives, we were wounded, fragile and extremely vulnerable and we depended on each other from the very start. We quickly became inseparable, very co-dependent on each other and we just needed that comfort of a fun, smiley face to weather the storm.

Every morning, after breakfast and before the therapy started, the patients were allowed to all get together and conduct their own meeting in the main hall. There was a piano and some musical instruments to entertain ourselves and just hang out and have some bonding time. It was a casual, social situation and most of the time we just goofed about, had a laugh and compared our war stories. It seemed to me, amongst the men especially, it was a pissing contest on who was the most badly behaved prior to coming in.

Tara and I had one thing in common, other than being British we just loved to make people smile, it was just our thing. One morning we decided to play a trick on the whole group. By then we all knew Tara could play the piano beautifully; she was always on the damn thing playing some incredibly complex concerto or another. I told her I wished I could play like her, and she came up with an idea so I could feel what it was like. She told me we were going to do a duet. We practised a short piece and decided that if I sat furthest away from the audience, she could block their view and make it look like we were both seriously talented concert pianists. It was genius. When we sat down to play for everyone the next day they were totally in awe. We played the most beautiful piece, well Tara did, and I was basically faking the whole thing, head back, eyes closed, really getting into it, when really, I was just plonking my fingers quietly on the keyboard pretending to play. As Tara's hands flew all over the place, up and down the keyboard, she created a masterpiece with elaborate flair that came so naturally to her. At the end, the crowd went wild, and we stood and took our bows. No one ever knew I could not play a note, it was brilliant. My beautiful friend made me feel so special and even though she knew my deepest darkest secrets, insecurities and shame, she loved me anyway, unconditionally.

The other inmates in our crowd were recovering drug addicts (albeit very rich ones — cocaine seemed to be the main problem). There were sex addicts, investment bankers, musicians and a whole cast of characters who were kind of cool and pretty glamorous. I was a little out of my depth and felt kind of stupid when I was asked what I was in for, as if we were hardened criminals doing time. Kind of hard to admit that I had a failed IVF attempt and had a complete mental breakdown in the shower! Jesus, I sounded ridiculous. Apart from the pills on the plane I was not on anything but a glass too many of champagne now and then and even that was extremely rare. Fortunately, no one seemed to mind that I was the drug dud of the group because I had a British accent and a super cute British best friend in with me, who everyone wanted to get to know as she was just so much fun!

Unfortunately, Gary did not have the same excitement over my newfound buddy as I did and his response on our next call was surprising. The story of Tara being in The Meadows had hit the headlines back home in London and he was not happy we had become besties! He warned me that there were aerial shots of the facility and helicopters would be flying over, so I was not to lie by the pool with her; the last thing he needed was his wife being pictured with the biggest party girl in London who had a drug problem, and I would be suspected of the same. So, true to form and typical of me when anyone tells me to do something, especially if they were in my bad books, I did the exact opposite of what he recommended and trotted straight back out to the pool with Tara for another sunbathing session and to get my ass kicked at ping pong yet again. Funny I was not 'That Ann' any more who was a bad influence; I was the good girl.

The six weeks flew by, and we nervously started to gear up for family week. In some ways we were excited to see our families but also pretty much dreading the whole thing and what we may have to confront. I seriously could not think of anything worse. The thought of my whole family getting together in one room sounded like hell on earth. This had not happened since I was about seven years old, and I was not down to have that experience again. It has always been times like this that I wished I had a nice normal family. Unfortunately, both my parents accepted Gary's invite to come out and support me. He thought it was important. I had the feeling of impending doom. This was going to be a shit show and I didn't think that Gary or any of the staff here knew what they were inviting into our calm, tranquil space. It certainly didn't do anything to cheer me up.

On the whole I had been making great progress. I still had trouble sleeping but was now putting together how my hormones crashed after IVF and how it had impacted my entire body and mind. During the second week you are given an assessment to review and a list of things that you were being diagnosed with so that you could learn about them and know which therapy classes you were supposed to attend. I apparently had about thirty things on my list, most of which I had never heard of. Tara had her list too and so we compared them. Not that you were allowed to do this, but we were not ones for playing by the rules and as we looked down at the names of illnesses on the pages, we realised our 'lists' were almost identical.

Now how could they have come up with this same list for two people with completely different issues? I was puzzled as I looked down the list of strange psychiatry terms, none of which even had a definition or explanation. I was apparently an alcoholic. I had never seen anything more stupid in my life. Yes, I liked a drink and now and then I took it a bit too far, but this was not a habitual daily situation that I felt was out of control. Trust me, I had friends who were batshit crazy alcoholics and I did not relate to that at all. Apparently, this diagnosis had come about due to my drinking on the day of the incident when I had the panic attack. It was explained to me I may be a binge drinker and lost control during those moments. Erm, actually no, that did not fit at all. My drink was spiked and that made my reaction to alcohol on that day amplified. But of course no one knew that at the time.

Not surprisingly everyone at The Meadows had one thing in common and that was some form of sedative or psychiatric medication was necessary and prescribed. Most of the time we did not even know what we were being given; we would just line up and take them morning and evening. I hated taking pills and did a great job of faking taking them. I kept them in my hand and made a collection of them back in my room. We were given the pills in tiny containers, so nothing was labelled or named or explained to us. We just did what we were told. Everyone left with a cocktail of antidepressants and sedatives to help us transition back into the real world. Gary and I both agreed psychiatric drugs were bullshit. I am truly thankful for his protection during this time. He gave me a new viewpoint on psychiatry, and I felt very strongly that I could heal without them through support and counselling.

Now what is interesting about all this was that not one single person clicked that I had just finished IVF and that the hormone injections I had been taking on a daily basis had finished. No one made the connection to the fact that this was playing havoc with my mind and body. Even I did not understand the significance until years later when I hit menopause and found myself having the same panic attacks and insomnia came to visit once again. That is when I made the connection. In hindsight what should have happened was, instead of being sent to a treatment centre, I should have been sent to hospital. I needed an endocrinologist and a blood work check out for my hormones and perhaps some counselling and support for the huge loss I had just suffered. None of that happened, it was all just brushed under the carpet and only I was cognizant of the pain that a life without children of my own would bring.

Over the six-week programme, I had good days and bad days and those days when seriously everyone needed to just keep their distance and not speak to me! New people came and went, and Tara made friends with a curly-haired musician called George. Tara and George started hanging out together and had to keep it under wraps, as it was against the rules. The plan was to get together when we all got out and see what happened. I didn't really talk to George that much; the scruffy musician type was not something I was interested in, and I didn't really trust that he was one hundred percent genuine. I think he got a bit swept away with who Tara was and the life she led. He was one to watch for sure.

Family week arrived and we were excited to see our families. We would not see much of each other during that week as it was a packed schedule, and we would have our hands full. Lunch time we would see each other at our tables with our families and we got a chance to catch up in the canteen as we lined up for food. Tara ran into the cafe on the first day, as I was queuing with my dad for lunch, she was carrying a massive bouquet of yellow flowers. She trotted around excitedly showing them to us, telling anyone who would listen that they were from her godfather Prince Charles. They came with a card, and she was thrilled. I was happy for her as it must have been nice to know he cared, even though she was in a bad situation. My dad however was not so impressed and quickly shot back, "Oh a little bit of name dropping is it, Tara?"

She laughed and looked him straight in the eye and said, "No, Darling, it's a big bit of name dropping." I was floored. She was not scared of him at all, and he thought it was hysterical and he laughed along with her. For the first time in my life, I had seen someone give my dad some lip and get away with it.

Of course, she was stunningly pretty, and my dad was a major flirt, but in that moment, she gave me confidence with him. Instead of treading on eggshells trying to think of the right thing to say to make him happy, usually I said the wrong thing and just pissed him off and the whole thing backfired. Tara helped me overcome that paralysing fear in that brief moment.

Tara's family were absolutely lovely. Her mum was just a sweetie and I loved that she was so down to earth, without any airs and graces, just a proper mum. Tara told me how lovely Camilla was and how funny and normal she was and how much happier Charles was since he had divorced Diana. I usually felt pretty inadequate around her; I think most people did as she lit up a room with her smile and incredible personality. She had something about her that made people just want to be in her presence. If I had a particularly tough day, she was the first person to cheer me up. We did art classes and my drawings of stick men looked like a three-year-old had gone nuts on the paper, whilst Tara casually knocked out these amazing fashion drawings of me in different outfits. They looked straight out of a magazine and were beautiful. She was so talented in so many ways and so underestimated and incorrectly presented in the media. It was so frustrating.

The first session of family week was about to start now that everyone had arrived and been given a warm welcome. Everyone was there for me, except my brother Marc, who was not allowed to fly on doctor's orders due to his heart issues, but he sent me a beautiful card that told me to just calm down and get control of my mind, which was exactly what I needed to hear and gave me strength to do what I had to do. As I knew it would, my family blew the place up. It was total chaos. My parents were arguing from day one; they hated each other. Gary was stepping in and trying to be the referee, as the counsellor was totally out of her depth. Most of my family had staged a walkout and refused to carry on unless someone else came in to lead it. Threats of people flying home were being bandied about and we were all in a state of fear and shut down, as all the triggers and unresolved problems of our past flared up once more. They were just so hard to confront and had never been talked about by any of us. I ended up in tears, retreating to my room just wanting it to stop.

I was very fortunate that the famous Pia Mellody had heard about our terrible day and had stepped in to take over the facilitation of this fractious group of strong people. She skilfully got us all back on track; we were way too scared of her to act out any more. She was very intense but amazing and handled my father in a way that he could be there and not lose his shit every time mother opened her mouth to contribute something to the group.

Our family week continued over the next few days, and everyone was able to air their grievances, which was hard, but so healing. It is a shame that my failed IVF attempt was swept over and talked about only briefly in private as Gary and I made the decision to not try any more and work on our marriage which was hanging by a thread due to various issues on both sides. By the end of the week, we had all come to an understanding and were in better communication and closer than we had ever been, except my parents who still hated each other, but at least we have a photograph of us all together for the very first time. We looked like soldiers who had been through war, but we had smiles on our faces at last.

Many things were addressed; my childhood, the violence, the last time my dad hit me when I was twenty-two and had just got back in touch with him. I got smacked around the head so hard my ears were ringing, all because I dropped a bowl of cream in the kitchen whilst making him dinner. During my session with my dad, I told him that if he ever hit me again or even raised his hand, it would be the last time he ever saw me. He apologised and I could see he had real tears and remorse.

Tara had a very different experience during her family week. Her parents were still married, and she got on really well with her sister. She talked about her diagnosis and recovery programme. She said one thing that struck me and that was that her counsellor thought she was addicted to fame. Was this even an addiction? Apparently, they felt, the more attention she got the more she craved and the adoration in the press and public was her way of finding acceptance. The trouble is with that, as many a celebrity has found out for themselves, the build-up is great and when they love you, they love you, but it was a double-edged sword and they could destroy you just as quickly with their words. It seemed like many of the paparazzi and tabloids were just waiting for her to fall from grace when she got out. It was a scandal when she admitted she was drinking again the occasional glass of wine, but she was not an alcoholic; that was not her downfall so why shouldn't she have a glass of wine? It annoyed me whenever I read anything negative about my beautiful friend.

Just before we waved our families off, Tara's mother read me a poem she had written for her daughter about a little girl on a carousel and dedicated it to her new friends. It basically compared living in the fast lane to being at the fair and getting stuck on a carousel. It was, of course, an analogy of what happened to her beautiful daughter, who had stayed too long at the party, and it was no longer fun. I really related to it and asked her for a copy, and she kindly gave me my own. I treasure it along with the beautiful drawings Tara sketched of me in our therapy sessions. Finally, our families left, and we had one more week to spend finishing our treatment. We had all laughed, cried and told each other our darkest secrets. We could not help but quietly wonder who would make it once back in the real world. I had total faith that Tara would be one of the winners.

I have wonderful memories of our stay. From saving a baby bird that had fallen from a tree and hiding it in our room, taking turns sneaking away from class to feed it, to our last night at The Meadows which will remain with me forever. We were taken to the desert, to a fire that had been built for us and as we sat on the ground, we had a ceremony with our American Indian spiritual guide, who was an incredible man. I certainly had changed from the first time he saw me, falling out of the limo on arrival. As the sun went down and the stars came out, we looked up to the sky and recited the serenity prayer. We then shared our future hopes and dreams and burnt notes we had made during our darkest moments. This was all in the past, the future was ours and although our time in this strange place was at an end, we were excited to be moving into the next chapter of our lives and grateful we had been so fortunate to meet each other and heal our wounds.

Arriving back home in Richmond six weeks later was a very strange feeling. Having been in a safe cocoon in Arizona for so long, I was nervous about getting back to my old life, especially now having children was a subject that was off the table.

I kept myself busy the first few weeks with therapy groups locally and started to rebuild my life. I used the communication tools I had learned in Arizona and made sure I was around positive people, who supported me rather than tore me down and judged me. I had to lose a lot of people who were toxic.

Gary and I were back on track, trying to work things out, but it was strained of course and then a bombshell was dropped in my lap, completely out of the blue. Gary had purchased a house in Hampshire, whilst I was away in The Meadows, and we were moving within weeks. His friends all loved fly fishing and lived on the River Test, and it was his dream to do the same, so he found a property in Hampshire near them, and the deal was done. Before I had time for my feet to touch the ground, I was packing up my home. Not exactly the ideal scene for me as I needed stability not to relocate to a remote village in the middle of nowhere.

When Gary drove me down to see our new home for the first time, I was very nervous, as it was an hour and a half from where we lived and pretty remote. Plus, I knew absolutely no one and Gary had explained he would be living in London during the week. I started to have the feeling that I was getting dumped in the countryside and it felt like a punishment. I literally felt the ridges between us and knew there was no way this would heal, because this decision had already been made. It was not even a discussion or negotiation.

Southington Mill was the first house on the River Test, which is the largest privately owned chalk fishing stream in Europe. As we pulled up outside and parked near the tennis court, I had to admit, it was the most beautiful place I had ever seen. It was not a huge, obvious new build but a quiet home tucked away, off the beaten track. You would never have found it, unless you knew it was there.

As we walked through the little wooden gate and over the arched bridge to the front door, you could hear the water rushing. It was heaven. I started to feel this might just be a good idea after all. A fresh new start and healing for us both, so we were now both excited and fully onboard. We moved in before we even sold Richmond; we just wanted to be out of London and in our safe haven, with our dogs, cats, parrots and my horse Paddy.

The sky was full of stars, as there was little light pollution, and my dogs Harvey and Beans could run around chasing rabbits and squirrels. It was magnificent and I soon fell in love with it as much as Gary did. The renovation would be an immense undertaking because it was listed, and everything had to be done with careful consideration and in keeping with the history. Even the grounds were SSSI protected, and we were very aware that it was the village treasure. I could also have my horse nearby which was a bonus. For years I had owned Paddy, my thoroughbred ex-racehorse and I spent hours commuting to ride him on the weekends. So, Overton had lots of opportunities to have him nearby and I quickly made friends with a local farm, and they offered to have him board there. It was only three minutes from my house and a perfect solution.

The Richmond house sold quite quickly, and we used the profit to begin the task of decorating our new home and had big plans. I loved the whole process, and did not even mind having up to twenty builders in the house every day, and a kitchen in pieces. To be honest, I was in my element with my dogs and horse nearby. I got used to being alone and eating dinner on my own every night in the kitchen and spent my time with our housekeeper Sue and river keeper Neville to keep me company. I had no real idea this would be the worst possible thing for Gary and I and our marriage and that we would completely drift apart. In reality I do not think we ever got over what happened after our IVF. We were both still hurt over it, and we just started living different lives altogether.

On a good note, my father often came down to The Mill to keep me company during the week. I loved making him lunch in the garden or running to the Orvis store in Stockbridge, so I could spoil him with even more fishing gear. I had spent years fishing with my dad as a kid; it was one of the few times he was truly happy and at peace during those long summer days beside our favourite lakes in Kent. He would show us children how to catch worms in the garden, by getting warm, soapy water and putting it on the grass and then we would wait for the worms to come up for air and grab them and put them in a container for bait. Poor things — I used to feel terrible for them, but I had no time for sentiment if I was to impress my father with my bait-catching skills.

My siblings and I kind of hated fishing; it was boring really but it got us out of the house and stopped us from being bored. God knows how my father kept us under control. I once got into trouble for putting maggots in my sister Kay's sandwich or throwing a worm in her hair. She would scream blue murder at me for that and had a lifelong hatred for worms that never went away. I was such a horrible little sister and made her life hell at times, but she still loved me. We laughed about that for years afterwards, well at least I did anyway.

Fly fishing was new to my dad and he was eager to learn. Of course, he was a natural and got very good at it, very fast. He even started to prefer it to his coarse fishing after a while. I had picked up some good casts over the years, including a decent double Spey cast, which I taught my father. Those were idyllic days where we fished all day and watched *Only Fools and Horses* at night, laughing our heads off at Del Boy's antics. It was bliss. So much healing had been done in Arizona. My father was my hero in so many ways; I guess it is the same for most girls. I respected his brilliant mind as a mathematician. He had such a boyish sense of humour and would laugh like crazy over the stupidest things. He was quick-witted and had a banter that cracked me up. He was calmer now for sure; life had kicked his ass more than once and he was finally able to relax. Don't get me wrong, he still had an edge and did not take any shit from anyone. He was still very direct and to the point, but he did not scare me any more and that was the game changer.

The other great thing for me was that my dad and Gary got along so well it just made life so easy. Life at The Mill carried on at an idyllic pace. My father would constantly be taking pictures; he still loved photography. He would proudly return home from a visit to show my grandparents the images of the garden. My grandmother once said to him, well if they cannot be happy there then they won't be happy anywhere. Such true words.

The millennium came and for New Year, Gary and my dad had decided it was time for a firework display. I thought this was a really bad idea, having been nearly blown up by fireworks last year in Lake Charles, Louisiana, whilst visiting Gary's mother Concetta. Gary's twin brother Grant was also there, and fireworks were a tradition not to be missed. As the clock got close to midnight, the boys made us all stand in the front garden and Grant held a rocket in his bare hands and lit it. Unfortunately, instead of going straight up, it took a detour and headed straight for the bush I was standing by with his mother and he nearly blew us both up. We screamed as it exploded, which the boys not only thought was hysterical, but Gary had filmed the whole thing. More of the same continued until I went inside, choosing to live instead of die. I must say we replayed the video a million times that night, laughing our heads off. So, you can understand my reservation when the word firework and Cardone are said in the same sentence.

Back at The Mill, we all went to the firework store near Basingstoke, to stock up with gunpowder. Gary and my father were taking this very seriously. Gary had drawn a diagram, not quite up to my father's draughtsman standards, but it would do, and I watched as they were like two kids in a candy store, picking out the biggest and the best fireworks they could find. Anyone would think they were planning to blow up the Houses of Parliament from the sheer quantity of gunpowder that they thought was needed. An hour later and finally ready to check out, the shop assistant gathered everything together and then he asked us how many people were attending the demonstration we were hosting, as he might like to swing by. We all laughed our heads off as it would just be us in the back garden and we were still worried we did not have enough! Later that day Gary spent the entire afternoon laying out the great display. He did not let my dad help, as he wanted it to be a surprise and impress him. Of course, my dad was a control freak, so he stood nearby, pretending not to watch him, totally thinking Gary was going to cock it up.

After dinner we took our garden chairs and put them right next to the lake and sat watching as Gary made the final adjustments to the great display. It was bloody cold, and a few minutes passed so Dad and I started rudely singing 'Why Are We Waiting', in true British style so Gary started to light the fireworks one at a time. The rockets were amazing, and the bangs were so loud we had literally woken up the whole neighbourhood. I could not see Gary for the sheer quantity of smoke billowing around but occasionally could make out his shadow as he ran from one firework to the next lighting them along the way and trying not to blow himself up in the process. It was the funniest thing we had ever seen, especially after each amazing rocket launched, my dad would shout out to him, "Is that all you've got" and laugh his head off as Gary ran to the next one to be lit. This went on for about an hour and was the silliest thing ever. Seeing my dad's happy face lit up by the unending battery of fireworks was the best thing ever. We were all laughing so much it became a moment I will never forget. The time and attention Gary gave my father was so needed, so welcome and will always be so greatly appreciated. Gary gave me confidence around my dad, and I felt safe which was a new thing for me to experience.

I settled into life in the countryside and was happy there with my dogs and horses although very lonely at times as I went to London less and less and only saw Gary when he came home for the weekends. This had all sounded like such a good idea when we moved but in hindsight, living apart was making us very distant. We were like ships in the night. Now and then I would go into London and Tara, and I would meet up. She was doing really well and had not relapsed which was a huge relief. It was now a year later, and we both had settled down in our lives and found an inner strength and peace. When we met, we mostly caught up on celebrity gossip, more than we talked about The Meadows; we both wanted to put that in the past and keep it in a special place in our hearts.

As I feared would happen my marriage fell apart, mainly from living in different locations most of the time and unresolved issues from The Meadows. I felt that I had not been heard as to my pain and sadness as to why the IVF had failed. I never had a voice and took the blame for it all. . Gary and I ended up going our separate ways which was very sad. In hindsight I was never able to get past the

149

nagging feeling that I just was not the one for him. My confidence had taken a massive hit with this thought always in the back of my mind and after some time apart he called and asked me to take part in marriage counselling in California. I jumped at the chance hoping that we could mend what was broken and as Gary was now living in San Diego, I hopped on a plane full of hope and love for him. I was not ready for it to be over; there was still too much love there. He thought if we could really look over everything, lay our cards on the table and be sure we were doing the right thing it would all work out much better than a snap decision. Grant was super sweet, and we all stayed at his house on the beach in La Jolla. It would be fair to say, by this time Gary had been involved with other people and so had I, but something kept bringing us back together and we wanted to figure out what that was.

To say the counselling was a nightmare would be an understatement. It was held downtown in San Diego and when I arrived for our first session, I noticed a blonde girl sitting in the reception area. She actually looked a bit like me, just shorter and very American. I had this horrible intuition hit me that she was one of Gary's new friends and I was totally right. Funny how a woman's intuition is so accurate sometimes. It is amazing we do not trust it more. I had a history of being spookily accurate and I had learned to listen to my inner voice.

Turns out the blonde was called Carol and was his new girlfriend. He had not even said a word, but it was just so obvious. Over the next few days, she started turning up everywhere and clearly wanted me to know who she was. It was the little things like calling him constantly for lunch whilst she knew I was with him, leaving her golf clubs in the back of his car, so she had to come and meet us to get them, it was endless. I sensed in her a sly confidence that she was just waiting for him in the wings, and I was not wrong, she clearly knew she had already won.

In true Annie style I decided to tackle the issue head on and called her, the conversation was awkward to say the least, but I just told her plainly and simply that I did not care if Gary had been dating her, but it would be greatly appreciated if we could continue our counselling without any more interruptions or appearances from her. I wanted us to have some space, to go through our process and figure out what we wanted. If he wanted to be with her at the end of it, so be it; I was not going to get in the way. She listened but was rude and dismissive. She told me that I obviously did not understand people could be friends. Yeah right!

The very next morning there she was again, as we were about to start our next session. It was full hair and make-up, tan on display in her cute outfit with her American uber white toothy grin on show. Damn, she really was pushing her luck. She walked past me and straight up to Gary and grabbed his hand. I just stood there shocked, as she giggled in his ear, "We are not supposed to be talking." WTF, she was really now taking the piss.

As she smiled at me and happily trotted off towards the bathroom, I decided that there was something about our previous communication that she had failed to understand, so I followed her, really wanting to know what the hell she was playing at. This was bullshit and after all, I am my father's daughter and I do not take kindly to being disrespected by people pushing their luck. I waited until she came out of the stall and asked her, calmly, if there was something she did not understand about our telephone conversation the previous day. Very confidently she turned to me, smiled and said, "If you cannot trust your husband, I suggest you get a leash." Clearly, I was being baited; she was enjoying the game and knew she had power over me so I did the best thing I could think of, and I walked away and headed out of the bathroom, just sick with the feeling she was not going to let us be. As I walked through the door, I felt a hand grab me roughly on my neck, and I heard her say, "You think you are so tough, don't you, Annie?" Okay, this was a big mistake on her part. Did she really think I was a pushover? Was she just that stupid? I guess because she was an athlete and did triathlons that she actually thought she was pretty tough but sadly she underestimated me completely, like so many before her.

She had made a big mistake laying a hand on me and this was now self-defence. Her hand was still around my shoulder when I turned around and hit her, not hard, just hard enough to get her to back off. She fell down for a second and I thought that was enough. I walked away again, and she came after me, grabbing a handful of my hair and started yanking my head around. Really, was she serious? Was this her best move? Everything was in slow motion, and I clearly remember having these thoughts as it was all happening. Was this a joke? Did she really think she would attack me and get away with it after torturing me for days flirting with my husband? I was suddenly very calm, and I grabbed her by the throat to get her to let go of my hair. It worked and so I put her up on the wall, so her little legs were dangling off the ground below and gave her my best right straight across her face. Jesus, that had been harder than I expected. Everything my dad had taught me came together in that one moment and I felt invincible. I truly connected to the energy and spiritual power within me, in a way I had never felt it before. My God, no wonder my dad liked to box.

Carol fell to the floor and just laid there so I calmly walked away and as I did, I noticed people were watching. Wow, I must have looked like a lunatic as I am sure they did not see the beginning of the fight and how that started but they sure did see the end. Wanting to give them an explanation of sorts, I turned back to Carol and said, "Next time go fuck someone else's husband. Mine does not need a leash." Game over. I was not proud of this moment at all and knew this had just ended my marriage for good, so she had won anyway.

Looking back on my childhood I had got into many scrapes in school of course and then there was all the karate sparring I had done which was just fun for me, but this felt different. It felt like justice and vindication momentarily. Gary soon heard what had happened, from her of course, and was absolutely furious with me. She was the total victim, bleeding in his arms and he was never told the truth of what went down. The marriage counselling was over. Carol and Gary were now firmly together; my actions had made the decision for him. He had zero understanding that I was being goaded by her for days before. He even asked me to apologise to her, which I did to please him. Deep down the only thing I was sorry about was that I had not hit her harder. She was the most passive aggressive, sly person I had ever met and if that is what he wanted then God help him, he was welcome to her. Gary and Carol left for Florida a few days later. Clearly, they were together, and I stayed behind absolutely shattered.

Devastated now my marriage was finally over, I called my dad and told him what happened. Of course, he wanted a blow by blow of the fight; not much had changed. After I relayed the story to him in detail, he called me stupid, thinking he meant hitting someone in America could be a legal nightmare, I was in agreement with him. But no, he had not meant that. He explained to me that if I had hit her properly the first time, she would not have pulled my hair. God, I loved my dad; the response of a legend!

I returned home to rebuild my life and had no idea where to begin. It would take five years to recover from my divorce. Five years for the nightmares to stop but during that time I found out who I really was, and this was worth everything. I spent those years in France working on myself and then moved to America for work and started to really get a sense of who I was and what I was capable of.

Gary remarried years later (not the girl in the fight LOL) and had two beautiful girls and I was genuinely happy for him as he had finally found his person and she was beautiful. His new wife was very intelligent and had life together, quite the opposite of me when Gary and I met, as I was very damaged and in many ways he helped me begin my journey of self-discovery and I learned something very important about myself after we broke up.

I was actually a giant. I had lived in the shadow of all the people I had been around for years believing I was not worthy and that the men I had relationships with were the important ones and so much better than me. My time alone taught me that was not the case.

7

Hormone Hell

The loss of a loved one is something everyone has to experience at some point in their life. No one escapes this. It is just the way it is meant to be. Trusting you are strong enough to survive the pain and grief of loss is really hard. For some people it is completely overwhelming and can send them on a path that is non-optimum for their own survival, triggering addictions and self-harm as a way to escape the pain.

You can try to avoid the pain and grief that is followed by the death of someone dear, but it never works as love is not a choice, it is a basic necessity of life and survival. I have spent my life searching for love and then running away from it as fast as I can before it consumed or destroyed me. Love still scares me to death, but eventually your past catches up with you and God, the universe, Mother Nature or some unexplained force has a way of stopping you dead in your tracks, mid-sprint and you suddenly have no choice left, but to take a long, hard look at your life, loves, losses and failings. This is commonly known as rock bottom. The good news about this phenomenon is that once there, the only way is up.

For me, the wake-up call came in the form of a text message, from my sister Kay asking me to call her urgently. Deep down I knew it was about my father. As terror gripped me, I pressed her number in Ireland and knew that he was either very ill or had already gone. I had spoken to him the day before and felt physically sick not knowing which one it was. The first words she said to me were, "Annie, are you alone right now?" And that was the moment rock bottom started pounding on my door. It turned out my father had had a massive heart attack and had died suddenly at home, overnight. He had been found by a neighbour as his dog Freddie was barking constantly the next morning, as he always did if my father went into diabetic shock and needed help or an ambulance.

I remember standing in the street, with the sunshine beating down on me, feeling myself collapse onto the sidewalk, whilst gripping the phone in one hand and holding on to my sweet dog, Foxy, with the other. As my sister continued talking, the overwhelm and sense of shock started to hit me. She stayed on the phone with me whilst I dragged myself to a friend's apartment and rang the bell. Thank God Jim and Keoni were home. That was the moment that stopped me in my tracks and changed everything.

I flew to England as soon as I could and as I walked into my father's apartment alone, I was shocked at the bloodstained bathroom carpet. It looked like a murder had been committed. No one warned me I would have to confront this. Apparently, he had gone into diabetic shock in the shower and fallen, severely cutting his head open. Like a detective I walked around looking at everything, picking up and reading his diary of his last moments, his last meal, his last blood sugar reading as it was all meticulously documented as usual, and I came to the obvious conclusion, that he was in a terrible state prior to his death. I felt overwhelmed with guilt that I had not been there for him. Kay had flown in from Ireland that morning and would be meeting me here soon to move everything out. Our older brother Marc came along as well and helped us take care of everything. Thank God he was there as I was only just holding it together and he had always been the voice of reason in my life and kept me grounded with his mature advice and outlook.

The funeral was the next day and had all been planned with the help of Kay's best friend Jill so the next day we all gathered at the crematorium, waiting for my father's hearse to arrive and my best friend stood with me basically holding me together. The anticipation of the day was so difficult, as I wanted to make a speech and talk about my father and how much love I had for him, but I was struggling not only with the loss but also the jet lag and lack of sleep. Why had I put myself under even more pressure?

To be honest, there were things that needed to be said and I wanted to make sure I was the one to say them. My siblings and I had all experienced very traumatic times with my father as children. It had been a very complicated and difficult relationship with him for us all and I wanted to say goodbye the right way. As I looked up, a long black car came into view carrying a coffin and I just lost it. I could not control the tears. I looked up again and Jill was walking towards me, so I tried to get myself together. She quietly said, "Actually, Annie, that's not your dad, that is the funeral before him. They are running a bit late today." A huge sense of relief came over me and I snapped out of grief and said, "Okay, thank you, Jill." My friend and I started to laugh with relief, seeing the funny side of it all. Then thirty seconds later, Jill came back over to us again and said, "So sorry, Annie, actually that is your dad." This was now officially ridiculous, and it set the tone for a very silly, very British funeral indeed.

My speech went as well as could be expected. I had always suffered with stage fright during school plays as a kid, but this was much worse. My emotions were all over the place. I had been there less than forty-eight hours. Blood was rushing through my veins as I stood up to the pew and to speak, everything was a blur as I just looked down at my piece of paper and tried to ignore the crowd staring at me. Somehow, I got through it and sat back down as quickly as I could. As I sat there with my eldest brother Marc, Kay and my younger brother Steven, we all realised this was our final goodbye. It was tough on us all, but we did what we had always done growing up; we were there for each other. Nothing needed to be said; our radar was still fully operational.

It was time for the last song and my sister had decided on my father's favourite musician to play him out. José

Feliciano was a beautiful guitarist, and my dad played his records constantly when we were young. As the first beats played out, I stopped in my grieving tracks, as I realised my sister Kay had only gone and chosen 'Come on Baby Light My Fire', at a cremation! I looked at her as if to say, "Perfect tune for a cremation, Kay, just perfect". By that time, we were all shaking with laughter. I thought the wooden pew was going to collapse. I just hoped the other mourners thought it was because we were crying not laughing! It was official; we were still the silliest family on the planet and my father would not have had it any other way.

After the service we all went back to have tea at Jill's house and our darling cousin Maria was with us. It was lovely remembering the good times, because sometimes they were hard to find in my memories.

Having said our goodbyes, I headed back to America as I only had a short time off work and the next six months passed so quickly. By May 2013 I came home again and just wanted to test the water and see what it would be like to live here again. Shortly after arriving, everything that could go wrong with my mental health did. Jet lag had impinged on me again and everything seemed to be speeding up and I felt as if my mind was glitching. I could actually feel the neurons fusing in my brain, which made a popping sound as it happened. It reminded me of how I felt in Arizona, after the IVF had failed, it was the same sleepless nights, confusion and brain fog. I had no idea that I was heading into a huge hormone crash and going into perimenopause and just did not have a clue. It sounds crazy but my mind was coming apart and I was struggling to remain calm. I had been working way too much and really burning the candle at both ends, trying to earn a living and establish myself, whilst studying as well. I was only getting about four hours sleep a night and it was building up into a perfect storm that I didn't see coming and could not stop.

For the next few days, I was completely lost, unable to sleep, unable to process simple communications, nothing made sense. I could barely recognize people I knew, and I had no concept of reality. I lost the ability to analyse and did not know if I was asleep or awake. It was all one big nightmare. The only way to describe it is like dreaming whilst you are awake. On the outside you look fine, but on the inside, you are going through hell as your mind is a muddle of lucid moments and then it would snap into a dream state. It left me trying to figure out what was real and what was not. During these first few days I was fortunate enough to have friends take me on long walks for hours, but even these did not wear me out.

This continued for a few days and nights. If I did sleep the dreams were vivid and whilst awake, I would try and make sense of them. Everything had significance and meaning behind it. I would look at someone or something and go into a calculation of what was similar and how it was all linked. Everything was linked, every incident, every vision led me down a path in my mind to another one. I just needed to be knocked out or else I was going to die. I felt I was that close by this time; my mind was exhausted and could not keep making insane computations at the speed it was running without causing brain damage. I was sure of it. Eventually in a moment of lucidity I called my mother and asked her to come and pick me up as I had been staying with friends. I was able to give her the address in those few minutes of sanity. Once she located me, she finally got me to a hospital, where I was sedated for two days. Thank God!

Waking up, I only had a vague memory of where I was and some recollections of how I got there. I was foggy but back to being me; exhausted but knew who I was and was totally back in present time. I had slept and that was all I had needed to stop the hell I was living through. I had no explanation at that time of what happened to me. I had no understanding that I had gone through a massive drop in oestrogen and was entering perimenopause. I had never even heard of the word like so many other women. I put it all down to lack of sleep, stress and was so humiliated. I tried not to think about it too much and focused on bouncing back and proving to those around me that I was okay and not completely fucking insane.

I was terrified that I had inherited some kind of severe mental illness but kept it to myself in the hope I was wrong. My thoughts kept flashing back to panic attacks I had experienced years earlier after I had IVF and my experience at The Meadows, in Arizona as many of the symptoms, especially the insomnia, was identical to what

I went through before. That is when I started to put two and two together and felt this was very familiar.

The symptoms I had been hospitalised for were exhaustion, dehydration, low blood sugar, raging insomnia and sleep-related psychosis, without having a clue how it started or where it came from. At the time I put it down to a complete nervous breakdown due to the stress of my father dying. When I woke up two days later, I felt better, more myself and not hallucinating, which had been horrific. My mind had played tricks on me, and I saw the edge of insanity, it literally felt like I was leaving my body and heading into another dimension. Landscapes would change from Summer to Winter right in front of my eyes and everything was a conspiracy as I felt dark forces were out to get me. This delusional state left me unable to comprehend what people were saying to me. Even having the television on was disturbing to me as I could not tell what was real and what was not. Everything had a hidden meaning whilst listening to the news. I was locked in hell and had no way of verbalising any of it. When I woke up from the sedation, I met with a team of psychiatrists who told me they were considering electroshock therapy! To say I was shocked (no pun intended) would have been an understatement. This was their idea of a solution for someone struggling with grief and lack of sleep. WTF was going on!

As I sat there listening to their recommendation, it all started to sound disturbingly familiar. The exact same thing happened to my father, during his second divorce in his late fifties. We were told he was suffering a 'breakdown' and had been sectioned by his wife who had full power of attorney. She gave her consent to him receiving twelve rounds of electroshock therapy.

Whilst he was almost left for dead, she spent his savings on a facelift (kind of gives you an idea of who she really was). His brother, David, was horrified when he saw him after the treatment. My father was drooling and could not speak; they had literally fried his brain. Uncle David could not believe what the doctors had done to his brother. For months he was unrecognisable and could barely form a sentence or remember words. It was inhumane. There was no way this was going to happen to me, and I became very agitated and verbal about it, which of course only made their case even stronger. Fortunately, I got it together and calmly thanked them for their 'care' and told them I was ready to leave. My saving grace was that my sister had made the journey from Ireland, to help bust me out of hospital. She knew history was trying to repeat itself and there was no way that was happening on her watch. It is only because of her presence, the fact she was medically trained and that we totally bullshitted our way out of there by saying I would stay with her, that they let me go. I drove home with Kay and my mother, packed my bags to go on a flight straight back to America. Fuck this for a solution.

For the next few years, I had so many questions about my father's mental health battles and started to compare them to my own. Was I mentally ill? Was this a one-off or would it happen again? Did I have dementia? Was my wiring completely off? What the hell was wrong with me? I was absolutely terrified and unable to face the full gravity of what had happened.

I studied, researched and questioned everything. By 2015 I had seen countless doctors and had huge amounts of medical tests, CAT scans, MRIs, blood work and incurred thousands in medical bills.

The only thing I came up with was it was time for me to stop running from life and finally face my past and go back and piece together what happened to my father and find out what was happening to me. There were way too many coincidences. It became an all-consuming obsession, as I tracked down and made each discovery one at a time and finally eight years later, the puzzle was complete, and the mystery was solved. My father had a hormone imbalance called diabetes. I had a hormone imbalance called menopause. We both were subjected to horrific abuse by psychiatry for this simple medical fact.

Two years later the same thing happened again, almost identical to the first one. The scary part was I had been fine for the time in between, working hard, no health issues, no warnings — just bang out of the blue I went south again, and I had no idea why.

The day started uneventfully but by the evening I was admitted to hospital completely delusional and suffering from dehydration. Earlier in the evening I had made the stupid mistake of locking myself out of my apartment. I had just taken a nap and woke up not knowing where I was. I walked out onto the street with the door closing behind me. I had no phone, no key and no way of getting help. Hours passed and I sat on the steps, my mind not being able to compute what to do. Occasionally people would go past but I would not tell them I was in trouble and just smiled as if I was waiting for someone.

I drifted in and out of reality and was probably suffering from exhaustion at this point. It felt like another few hours passed, and I needed to go to the bathroom. I started to walk up the street and managed to get up to the main road which was Sunset Blvd. A few homeless people wandered by, but no one paid me any attention. I must have looked like I fitted in quite well. I was a wreck; shoeless and now a bloodstained dress was really causing me to be embarrassed. Thankfully I realised right in front of me was the Kaiser Hospital and as luck would have it, I had insurance with them so I walked up to the reception but quickly found I really could not communicate what had happened. I remember pointing to my head, but they obviously thought I was on drugs or drunk or could have been having a miscarriage, so they got me up to the maternity ward as quickly as possible where I did a pregnancy test. Talk about getting it wrong.

I cannot remember much after this; I must have passed out completely. I woke up in an ambulance, handcuffed to the rails and was just confused. I was then transported to a psychiatric ward just as it had happened two years before and I still had no idea that in 2013 I was in a perimenopausal hormone crash and now my endocrine system had crashed again due to going into menopause. It was only due to an amazing doctor called Megan Shields who suggested I get a hormone test as soon as I left the hospital and sure enough, there it was in black and white, the numbers on the blood work indicated that I had zero hormones and that was the issue. I finally had the answer to what the hell was happening to me. I was not mentally ill, I was just one of the unlucky women whose menopause symptoms include insomnia and after about three to four nights of zero sleep, anyone would go batshit crazy. Finally with the beginning of some understanding it was now time to really start doing some research and find out what else lay in store for me and what I had to do to make sure I stayed healthy.

It turned out that the endocrine system is so complex and really is the communication channel that every command the mind gives the body goes through. It is so important yet so misunderstood it boggles my mind. General practitioners are not specialists in the field or the endocrine system and hormones. Nowadays if a woman in menopause goes to her doctor and tells her she is feeling depressed, cannot sleep, anxious or stressed, chances are she will be given antidepressants. It will not always be recommended she has a hormone test to check her levels, but the symptoms will be treated instead of the cause. The problem with that is psychiatric drugs are not a cure for menopause as they bring another set of symptoms such as: Suicidal thoughts, insomnia and depression.

After this event, my partner Dan and I decided it was time to stop having a long-distance relationship and that I should move to Texas to recover and take some time out, which never happened as I walked into a household that was full of drama. Dan wanted me to raise his four teenage daughters and that was fine by me. On a good note, I was finally getting some hormone replacement therapy and was excited to put this drama into the past and move on with living my life minus having a nervous breakdown every couple of years.

After checking out some local doctors and endocrinologists I found a clinic in Texas and the doctor re-checked my blood work and recommended a testosterone implant as that usually worked well for everyone. Having heard my girlfriends discussing it years ago, I felt at ease with the suggestion, and I had to put my faith and trust in the experts and reasoned they were doing this all the time, so it had to be okay. The implant was supposed to create some balance with my hormones. Instead of creating a balance and helping me sleep it had the opposite effect and within a few days I was a total mess. The testosterone made me tense and angry. I was aggressive, my sex drive went through the roof and trust me, your partner is not going to be attracted to you when you are in mean mode.

I also found the testosterone implant had some serious side effects. I felt so stupid for not researching that before, just blindly going ahead with it. Even worse, this was an implant and would now take up to three months to be out of my system. You cannot just take it out. When finally, the three months were up I was able to change the HRT to oestrogen and progesterone in the form of a pill. This, I was assured, would settle things down. The progesterone was amazing. I was put on quite a high dosage to begin with — 400mg and as soon as I took it, I would relax and fall into a deep sleep. Dan was with me in the car as we left the pharmacy with my new prescription and sat there in amazement, as I took my medication and within ten minutes, I was sleeping in the car like a baby for the first time in months.

Things were looking up. I was more relaxed, happier, coping better with my chaotic home life on the new hormone regime and Dan and I settled into a routine. The only blip on the horizon was one of the children was clearly in serious trouble with drugs and yet again the stress levels ramped up. The children's mother was completely absent at the time I arrived, but she agreed to meet with me, and I hoped she would have some insight as to what was going on with the kids. Clearly, we needed to all work together and there was no way I wanted to be on the wrong side of her as she still had way too much influence over them and not in a good way.

We met the next day at an Italian restaurant a short drive from the house and when I arrived, she was sitting at the table and seemed happy I had reached out. I am sure she had been told some stories from the kids from what happened in LA, and I was very conscious that I was the crazy woman Dan found who had just got out of a psych ward. I had no doubt she was fully informed. I had also been very well informed from the children on their childhood and how it was growing up, she liked her alcohol and having affairs way more than she liked being a mother. It was not a pretty picture, but I was open to making my own judgement.

We started off polite but after quite a few drinks I warmed up to her and thought this is someone I would actually be friends with. She was beautiful, cool, funny, kind of edgy but you could tell she was strong, and you could also tell she loved her kids. As she talked about the past and what went wrong in her marriage, she downloaded the whole story from her viewpoint. We were a few drinks in at this point, mainly due to being both a bit nervous in the beginning but we were bonding, and I liked it. Unfortunately, Dan did not come out looking very good as I listened to her version of events, and I guess it takes two, but I started to get nervous when some of the information about the man I loved became really unpalatable. I could not believe that this was the same man I was now in love with. There were very real reasons she had left that I could relate to, and she was either being really open and honest or she was really doing an assassination job on him. Yet again another layer of stress was added to my plate as in the back of my mind I heard her voice putting down the man I loved and almost willing me to get out whilst I still could. It was not helpful, that is for sure.

Not wanting to cause a problem I brushed off the lunch incident, got into action and started to handle the children and help them with their issues and tried to make their lives a better place. I had found an incredible endocrinologist who helped me understand the part stress played on the delicate balance of the endocrine system. She listened to my story and was not even remotely surprised I had been struggling. The children's issues alone would have sent anyone over the edge.

Dan was with me at one appointment, and she told him that he needed to minimise my stress and that these were his children and his responsibility and way too much for me at the time. He completely disagreed. He corrected her and said NO, they are her children, you need to understand that simple fact. He seemed to not get that his children had severe childhood trauma and the repercussions from this were running me into the ground as they offloaded their past memories on me on a regular basis and were on their own emotional roller coaster. Teenage girls are never easy, especially with their own hormones going all over the place. I was out of my depth. I had no idea how other parents managed teenagers, but it always seemed to work out that just as one child would stabilise, another started to kick off. Even though we had help, in the form of a family friend who was our cleaner, who was a complete joke as she had even done drugs with the kids in the past, it was never-ending. Apart from that there was no help as their mother wanted nothing to do with the day to day raising of her own children. I tried asking her to pick them up after school or take them to a dental appointment or a therapist and we would always get refused. She was too busy, yet she did not even have a job and totally relied on us to pay all her expenses.

I tried to ignore her lack of support and still invited her to Thanksgiving, Christmas and all the kids' birthday dinners. I did my best to make it go right and for a while it worked. I am not saying we were now best friends, but there were good times when the whole family were able to be together and have a great time. It was progress for sure. I had no idea at the time that I was dealing with an addict who hid the truth really well and only discovered her true state of mind when I went to her house to pick up one of the children. As soon as the kids got in the car, I noticed the smell of cigarettes; one of them literally smelt like an ashtray. I asked her if she had been smoking and she told me absolutely not. She hated that her mother practically chain smoked the whole time. In my usual bulldozer way, I wanted to deal with this straight away. I walked into the house and could not believe what I was seeing.

There were stained carpets from the dog that had not been cleaned up properly, overflowing ashtrays, food everywhere, dishes piled up in the sink and no counter space at all on view. It looked like a drug addicts' squat and smelt even worse. I quickly went back outside. I was horrified. No wonder these kids had zero clue about health, hygiene and keeping their home clean as their mother was incapable of looking after herself. It soon felt like Dan, and I had five kids under our wing as we tried to manage her as well. I believe she resented our interference if we confronted her over drinking around the kids and stuck her heels in even more and refused to be of any assistance. Even when she got wasted with one of the girls on their twenty-first birthday and made her child drink drive because she already had too many points, I had no way of letting her know how fucking irresponsible I thought that was. What kind of mother would put her child in harm's way to save herself? I was disgusted but by now I knew I had to keep my mouth shut because anything I ever said against her turned all the children against me and would start a war.

Their mother was a train wreck and I had no idea she was in this condition as she always looked very put together when I saw her but clearly, she was not doing well; she could not even look after herself let alone help with the children, even when we offered her help she turned us down, the only thing she wanted was her bills to be paid and money in her account to buy cigarettes and alcohol other than that she wanted nothing to do with us.

In fairness to myself as a stepmother, I had no manual to go by and was literally making shit up as I went along, and all I had in the form of experience was my own strict, messed-up, abusive, violent childhood. I honestly made so many mistakes and fucked up so many times with the kids, it was amazing they even liked me at times, but as time went on things started to slowly improve. Moving house helped for sure and I started to develop a stronger bond with the youngest child who was just adorable. I had started to actually have some fun and fortunately we had one thing in common: we were both obsessed with rescuing dogs and pets and basically anything fluffy and cute. I finally started to live the childhood I never had. We sang songs in the car, she shocked me with her crude rap songs that she would cheekily sing along to with all her friends piled in the back. Reversing out of McDonald's one afternoon, I smashed Dan's good car into a lamp post. God, I really was a crap step monster and the kids in the car agreed.

Dan worked crazy hours so was kept out of the loop of so much that went down, one time we even smuggled a kitten into the house, a big white fluffy one and kept him a secret for months. When Dan finally found it, he was livid but also thought it was hilarious. We did it again about six months later with a pug, and told Dan it was a friend's, and we were looking after it. Obviously, he caught on and by the time he did it was too late; the pug had us all in love with her. Poor Dan, we even celebrated Easter by getting rabbits; they became huge and even had their own room in the basement. We soon realised that two rabbits became about eight as they had children as we had accidentally got a boy and a girl. It was brilliant. We had so much fun, we seriously had a farm.

Meanwhile Dan and I set a wedding date. This crazy family was now becoming mine too and when the day finally came, I can honestly say it was so easy and smooth. We had one hundred people RSVP and as the day drew closer, I was excited that my sister would be making the long trip. Picking her up from the airport I could not stop hugging her. She would be one of the few people who made it to the wedding from my side; nearly everyone else attending were joint friends. Another person I classed as family flew in from LA and this was Katie. She was like a daughter to me and when we met years before in LA, we decided that we were family.

As I walked down the aisle with the song 'A Thousand Years' playing, I saw Dan completely lose it. He had his hands up to his face and was crying with happiness. It was so emotional. He could not believe we made it this far; we were both so excited for our future. We said our vows and the children joined in and we were married. The day went so fast and before we knew it, we were off on our honeymoon, aptly renamed our family moon in Mexico. I wanted to share every moment with the whole family as this was their success too. Little did I know that this moment would be fleeting and in hindsight I now realise that I had just created my past in my present. Here was my familiar childhood story of a single man struggling to raise four children whilst battling health issues. If it felt like I was home it was because that is exactly where I was, back all those years ago. Funny how we recreate the past and end up attracted to and comfortable with such dysfunction but that is all I knew and just like I did so many years ago I jumped in, where others would not and set about to fix up the whole family.

I was relentless in my quest to get everyone back on track, from home-schooling to creating a beautiful home and trying to make everyone's life better. I had no idea how to be a parent and so many times I messed up and went about things the wrong way, but my intentions were good. I had no concept of pacing myself and had no idea how to not worry about what the children were doing and what trouble they were getting into as there were no shortage of problems popping up constantly, but each time we got through them. To say Dan was a good father would be an understatement, he was a fantastic father who was so kind, patient, understanding and so full of love and the feeling of being responsible for making up the damage that had been done from his failed marriage, it was all he thought about. He had never, once, ever raised his hand to any of his children and that was wonderful for me to see. On top of that any of them could come to him and be honest about any situation in their lives or the trouble they were in, and he would just be so compassionate it floored me, I had never seen anything like it and had certainly never experienced it for myself and it made me love him even more. We were a formidable team without a doubt and slowly and surely, without any help from the children's mother we started to turn things around.

This is where the story line turns to 'and they lived happily ever after' but sadly that was not meant to be as six months later my health took a turn for the worse after a specialist at the hormone clinic changed me from an oral pill form of oestrogen to a cream and my hormones crashed to the floor. On top of this, Dan had been given another drug to help me sleep called Ambien and that was the final straw. About thirty minutes after being given Ambien, I was hallucinating, and an ambulance had to be called. Sadly the 'in sickness and in health' part of the vows did not hold true as it became a reality that our marriage would probably not survive my roller coaster heath issues. Trying to stabilise my hormones was now becoming a full-time job and my last episode and the constant stress this family created just was not conducive to my continued stability.

There is a reason why women have menopause, not men. I honestly do not think the male species would have survived it for a second. It is a brutal roller coaster of complex hormones that, when upset by stress, or when doctors make changes to my hormone medication, without advising me of the potential consequences, it really can become a fight of life and death and a test for those around you.

It is during these dark days that the proof of love really does come to the forefront, as each individual who is affected by someone going through this reacts in their own way and even though you have been there for others during the hardest of times and their own batshit crazy behaviour as they battle their own problems, there is no guarantee anyone would be left fighting for you.

If I had Alzheimer's or dementia, would it have been different, I wondered? Would my husband and his family have fought for me? And the answer is probably yes, and I would still have a family intact and a husband who loved me, but with menopause that is not the case. Outwardly you look fine but inwardly you are dying and there is not a damn thing you can do about it.

The sad part was that this family and I had been through so much together, we had so many victories including getting one of the children off crystal meth, another one was self-sabotaging and cutting, and that was getting better, but the good things and the victories got side-lined and the focus was on the fact that I was unwell and could not stabilise in this environment, but to be honest, I was up against some serious family dysfunction that would have sent most people over the edge. If the children's own mother had run away, unable to stay and fix the situation without losing her mind and turning to drugs and alcohol, how was I supposed to be the one to make it go right? Yet that was the expectation on me; I was not allowed to lose my shit yet everyone else around me was.

Understandably, my stepchildren were now not wanting to spend much time with me and the feeling was mutual. They kept their distance and were wary. I don't think they ever really fully understood that the problem was not just menopause but a perfect storm of stress and overwhelm which was playing a huge role. Only one doctor had concluded that the stress of this family was tipping me over the edge on a regular basis. The bottom line is though, it was my responsibility to practise self-care and not let anyone overwhelm me or affect me. To say no to all the demands and just take care of myself. I had never done this and had got to a time in my life where I had to, or I would end up dead.

Dan and I went through so much. How we survived every onslaught of problems one after the other created by the children I will never know. Every time we managed to keep our heads above water and handle all the issues with the kids together, but our marriage was not going to survive. My health problems had galvanised the kids with their mother, and they were all now against me.

I was lucky that my sister had come to help me after my last hospitalisation and she finally made me see sense, there was no way I could remain in this marriage. Dan and I were arguing, as he was insisting I leave and go home with my sister, which I absolutely did not want to do as I knew that would be medically the worst thing possible for me.

During this time, my sister witnessed, for the first time, how stressful my life was. I told her the truth of how life had been lately and how the chaos and drama was just never-ending and she begged me not to stay with them. It was unhealthy for me to be around such a toxic, dysfunctional group and she knew it. It was up to Dan and his ex-wife to sort their own kids out; it was not my responsibility at the cost of my health. It was time for me to step down and let them all get on with it. I even called my doctor to see what she thought about me travelling back to the UK to recuperate and she absolutely said travelling right now would be the worst thing I could do. The jet lag and time difference alone would severely interfere with my sleep patterns which could trigger another episode. To add to this, my sister's farm was two hours from the nearest hospital. If anything happened whilst I was there, I would be in serious trouble. Add to that she did not have a guest room. It was impossible but Dan and the kids did not even take it into consideration, they just wanted me gone. Dan said he needed to focus on work; he did not have time to look after me and he made that clear and that is where this relationship ended.

After I spent a few days resting and getting my strength together, I packed up the car with my dogs and headed back to California. Taking on an eighteen-hour car drive alone, having just got out of hospital, almost finished me off. How I did not fall asleep at the wheel I will never know but anything was better than staying after I read a nasty email one of the children had written with the help of her mother. I got the message and knew I was not wanted. Before I left, I had sent my sister the email and she begged me to get out of there. She could not believe I had been there for them through all their issues, and this is how I was repaid. She was done and told me if I did not divorce Dan, she would never speak to me again. She warned me, if I stayed, I would probably end up dead. She was very serious about it. She never spoke to Dan again. She never forgave him, and my darling girl was diagnosed with liver cancer shortly afterwards and passed away within six months and with her went a piece of my heart.

Like me, Kay was a person who always put everyone first. She loved life and she loved helping others. At her home in Caherdaniel, Ireland, she was known for speaking her mind, helping others and wanting to make a difference in the community.

Three years before she died, she had gone to the doctors with pains, and he had not taken them seriously enough and he did not send her for tests. So, she got on with it and suffered in silence and by the time they found out what was really wrong, it was too late. In her final months she started to take care of herself, putting herself first, resting and doing everything that was recommended with alternative therapies so she could live longer. Also, like me, her stress levels were always running high, and she never learned to relax and take time for herself. It was a product of our childhood where taking care of my father and each other was a full-time job and the priority.

I was fortunate enough to spend some time with her during her chemotherapy and we talked about why we both had these character traits of being comfortable with overwhelm and running our lives at one hundred miles an hour. It came back again to our upbringing and we both agreed we were comfortable with life at this pace, but it had to change if we were going to be well.

Kay passed away on the 28th of August 2019. Over five hundred people attended her funeral which was a testimony to how much she was loved in her community. Her children Amy and Dylan are her legacy, and the village will never forget her. She is the main reason this book was written; to make a difference. To encourage women to slow down at this time of life and change the pace. To stop taking care of people who can take care of themselves and to start listening to a body that is trying to tell you it cannot cope by manifesting illness. The body and mind has a way of forcing you to stop when you will not. We have to start noting that the warning signs are to be taken seriously or the consequences could be fatal.

I wish I could turn back the clock and have given my sister this message, encouraged her to take a breath but we both were conditioned by our traumatic past to go through life at warp speed, completely stressed and unable to stop for a second because if we did the memories of the past might have time to catch up with us.

It is true of so many survivors of abusive childhoods we just do not learn that we are important, and our only sense of worth is based on pleasing other people so we can stay safe, if someone is happy with you and you are indispensable then chances are they will treat you well and that is what we are working from and why we do not honour ourselves and make ourselves a priority.

Leaving Texas, Dan and his family was the best thing I could do to protect myself going forward. Cutting the ties with them all and leaving them to their own devices was so freeing as once I had distance and time, I had the gift of hindsight and realised Kay had been right all along, this was not my family, not my responsibility and no longer my problem.

8

Menopause is not a Mental Illness

Having been through so much during my menopause journey, the one thing I realized is this: your past catches up with you eventually. All the issues that remain unhandled in your life, which have caused you to feel less than and spurred you on to prove yourself start to resurface as you go through menopause. The days when you can get away with not looking after yourself and spend your time running at ninety miles an hour to make others happy and solve their problems are coming to an end as the stress this causes will start to bring you to your knees, which is a good thing really as life is meant to be enjoyed not raced through. It is at this time that your physical and mental health will start to break down and give you no choice but to change your operating basis.

It is only when you hit a wall in menopause and say enough is enough; it is time for change, then that is when you know things will start to get better, as they did for me. Hitting rock bottom was the only way I could start to climb back up and this was only done through finding value in taking care of me. Menopause is like a gift in so many ways as you realize the consequences of continuing self-neglecting behaviours are not worth risking and you start to understand how fragile you are and that you need to protect yourself from toxic people. My childhood was not easy for sure and although I take away some great lessons from it in hindsight, it also crippled me emotionally when it came to being able to love in a healthy way. I truly did not know how to have true intimacy and closeness with another person; it was just way too scary. Allowing people into your life and trusting they will stay was the hardest thing for me to learn, especially as there were more losses suffered as my hormones started playing up. People that I never believed in a million years, walked away and distanced themselves. People I had helped in their lives, through their problems over and over again, there was never a question in my mind that I would be there for them and there was never a moment when I thought I would one day be completely alone.

It turned out being alone was the best thing that could have happened to me. Living in a world where I only had myself to think about and take care of is what got me back to wellness. I did not have my attention on anyone except my sister's children and my mother and siblings. I would have given anything to have traded places with my sister and often wished I had gone too but that was not meant to be and maybe I still had this book to write for something good to come out of the hell I had lived through. It is strange how thoughts of death and dying can go through your mind during an endocrine crash. It was the same in The Meadows during hormone depletion. It is as though your mind cannot take anymore but you will not give up the fight for survival. These are not suicidal thoughts but just a desire for the pain to stop that so many women experience during the change.

Getting back to health meant studying the endocrine system, which was a struggle at first but the more I read the more I understood what had happened to me. The biggest clue was to understand the hormone levels and be able to interpret the numbers as a guide to my wellness. One of the biggest problems going through all of this was trying to explain it to other people. They just did not get it and almost wanted to put you in a box called "mental health issues" rather than try to see the truth of the situation.

When people have a visible illness then it is much easier for others to be empathetic, when it is a hormonal issue and invisible or beyond their limited understanding, they are less tolerant.

Confusion around hormone issues is rampant so it is not surprising that research shows that almost a third of women going to see their GP for issues with menopausal side effects are offered antidepressants. The worrying thing is that without enough information, understanding and education on this subject, many of them think that this is the only option and will do anything to relieve their symptoms of hot flushes, insomnia, headaches, anxiety, brain fog, mood changes, vaginal dryness, low libido and sadness. It is not surprising they will do anything the doctor tells them in the hope of feeling normal again.

How have we allowed things to get this bad? Lack of education in this area leaves women susceptible to this injustice and before they know it, they are on highly addictive medication which will rob them of their lives. Many of these antidepressants have suicidal tendencies as a side effect. Now tell me, how is that better than hot flushes? How is it possible that we are tolerating this? Sadly, this is not just happening to women in menopause, but also women who go through childbirth are victims of the system, including a family member of mine who lost her life whilst dosed up on psychiatric drugs that she had been prescribed for post-natal depression. Her little boy was only four weeks old and in the same room when she hung herself.

Here is a list of current antidepressants prescribed for women during menopause as a solution to the issues they are having in their mind, as doctors often overlook the fact that these women are having endocrine crashes and the issues can be hormone related:

Lithium: prescribed for menopause related depression.
Side effects: headaches, nausea, diarrhoea, dizziness, drowsiness, hand tremors, dry mouth, increased thirst, change in heart rhythm. If the dosage is too high it can cause severe toxicity and cause kidney failure, low blood pressure, coma, seizures, delirium and death.

Xanax: prescribed for depression, anxiety and panic attacks.

Side effects: drowsiness, tiredness, dizziness, sleep problems (insomnia), memory problems, poor balance or coordination, slurred speech, trouble concentrating, irritability, diarrhoea, constipation, increased sweating, headache, nausea, upset stomach, vomiting, blurred vision, appetite or weight changes, swelling in your hands or feet, muscle weakness, dry mouth, stuffy nose, loss of interest in sex.

Effexor: prescribed for depression.

Side effects: nausea, drowsiness, dizziness, dry mouth, constipation, loss of appetite, blurred vision, nervousness, trouble sleeping, unusual sweating.

Prozac: prescribed for depression, eating disorders, panic attacks, obsessive compulsive disorder.

Side effects: suicidal thoughts, decreased libido and sexual dysfunction, anxiety and nervousness, abnormal dreams, sweating, diarrhoea, asthenia, or lack of bodily strength, skin rash, tremor, flu syndrome, insomnia, drowsiness, and yawning, sinusitis, an inflammation of the mucous membrane, painful or difficult digestion, known as dyspepsia, dry mouth, nausea, vasodilatation, or widening of the blood vessels.

Ambien: prescribed for sleep disorders and insomnia.

Side effects: hallucinations, amnesia, hypnosis, memory problems, sleepwalking, sleep driving, rapid heartbeat, nausea, vomiting, dizziness, weakness.

So, looking at this list of drugs that are prescribed to women during menopause, can you imagine how insane the whole concept is that these medications could make them feel better? Surely a blood test to check out the hormone levels would make more sense as a first step. It strikes me as very odd that so many of the prescription drugs have the side effect of insomnia and sleep disturbances and insomnia was the whole reason doctors tried to get me to take these drugs in the first place and thankfully, I declined. It was only after I was given Ambien that I got a taste for myself how dangerous the effects of these drugs are, within hours I was hallucinating out of my mind and an ambulance had to be called. I was then taken to ER, and due to the fact I was hallucinating because of the drugs I had been put on, I got sent to a psychiatric ward. So, I was diagnosed based on the side effects of the drugs I had been given that were supposed to help me. Now how does that make any sense?

Clearly there is a correlation between menopause and the negative impact it has on the mind, but surely the obvious path to take would be to do blood work and balance the hormones, not to prescribe toxic drugs that are addictive and so dangerous but of course blood work and testing takes time and costs money so therefore psychiatry benefits because we all fall into the mental illness category as anyone would if they had spent four nights without sleep. In fact, this cannot even be proven because it is too dangerous to run experiments to produce the statistics. The fact is people can go insane or die from lack of sleep. Insomnia is one of the dominant side effects of menopause so you can see how easily we can get caught up in the dark world of psychiatry, we are such easy prey due to this simple fact.

When you look at the range of symptoms for the high and low of each hormone you can see why we feel so bad as they go up and down in life.

Low oestrogen: shifts in mood, hot flashes, headaches, depression, painful sex, increase in urinary tract infections, irregular or absent period.

High oestrogen: bloating, swelling, insomnia, fibrocystic lumps in your breasts, decreased sex drive, PMS, mood swings, headache.

Low progesterone: bloating, Anxiety or agitation, fatigue, depression, low libido, weight gain.

High progesterone: irregular periods, infertility, mood changes, anxiety, depression, fibroids, weight gain.

Low testosterone: sluggishness, muscle weakness, fatigue, sleep disturbances, reduced sex drive, weight gain.

High testosterone: excess body hair, balding, acne, deepening of voice, increased muscle mass.

Low serotonin: anxiety, depressed mood, aggression, insomnia, impulsive behaviour, irritability, low self-esteem, poor appetite.

High serotonin: confusion, agitation, muscle twitching, sweating, shivering, diarrhoea.

Low cortisol: headache, body ache, fatigue, nausea, sweats and chills, racing heart, high or low blood pressure, depression, anxiety, confusion.

High cortisol: weight gain, mood swings, increased anxiety, fatigue, high blood pressure, excessive thirst, acne, muscle aches and pains.

Looking at the list above makes you realise that the doctors are diagnosing people with a mental illness when it easily could be a high or low hormone issue and then when you add to this the balance between the hormones and how that comes into play, and you start to see the chances of feeling better in menopause are very slim if we do not bring down the stress levels. Cortisol became the most important hormone for me to tackle first and get under control and the only way to do that was to handle the stress in my life and start cutting down the things that added to it. I changed my life completely and started to become very protective of who I allowed into my space and stopped rescuing people who mainly were causing their own problems.

Going back to the vulnerable women who go to their GP for help, over seventy-nine per cent of them did not even get their questions answered regarding the menopause and other options available including HRT. In all honesty, my own GP admitted he knew very little to nothing about menopause as it was not his area of expertise, and it is this lack of education that makes the GPs the bad guys as they are not educated enough to make a difference and help these women. It would not take much to change the way doctors are trained to include the endocrine system, as clearly there is a high demand in their constituencies for solutions to this problem. Giving out highly addictive drugs to women who are coming for help is pure irresponsibility and no better than a street pusher in my viewpoint. Sadly, doctors can now elect not to take classes on menopause, it is not even compulsory.

It is only when you have walked a mile in the shoes of a woman who has suffered as I have that you can begin to understand what we are dealing with. Having shared rooms in psychiatric wards with these women and heard their stories it was impossible for me to do nothing about it. I was one of the lucky ones as I was always out of the hospital as soon as they allowed me to take my HRT, even though I had to fight for days to get permission. Astonishingly they were happy to tranquillise me every night with highly addictive medication and then wonder why I was not sleeping due to the fact they do fifteen-minute checks all night and shine a torch in your face to make sure you are alive. The logic really is astounding. So many women I met were not so fortunate and ended up on these wards for weeks and months. From there they would be court ordered to a county hospital for six months at a time, and once you are in that system it is very hard to get out. You basically have no rights and no life. You are told what to eat, what to drink, when to sleep and turned into a compliant zombie with a cocktail of prescription pills. This could all be prevented by a simple hormone test and access to a specialist who can interpret the blood work and help these women. It seems strange that no one is taking notice in the medical profession that a high percentage of these women have just given birth or are in the menopause age range. You do not need to be a doctor to notice this basic fact.

I have met women in psychiatric wards whose lives have been taken over by the mental health system and are no longer in a position to make decisions for themselves. They have lost their children, their husbands, their homes, their jobs, their health and their sanity, all for the sake of a hormone test that they could not afford and therefore fell prey to the pharmaceutical industries that have a one-size-fits-all solution for everyone. I will never forget their faces or their stories and often wonder what happened to them. Did they eventually walk free?

My hope in writing this book is to bring about understanding in this field. I am no doctor, but I do have enough experience on the receiving end of the treatment available to women in menopause to be able to form an opinion and take a stand over what I believe is abuse of our basic human rights. Simple education is needed if we want to bring about understanding to those in the medical field and those suffering and also lead to empathy from loved ones who are at a loss. Education is the only way to a stronger support system for those who suffer. I have never felt so alone in my life as I did through this experience, and I want to say to every woman who is going through this that I understand how you are feeling in a way that people who have not been through just cannot. My story is not uncommon, but it is usually kept a secret as we are humiliated and confused about what happened.

Just know you are not just crazy, but a human being with a compromised endocrine system that is affecting your body, mind, emotions, thoughts and feelings. Just knowing this brings a great deal of relief from the suffering.

There are days that sometimes you just need a hug and for someone to say, "I love you; we have got this, we will figure it out", and give you the reassurance that they are not going anywhere. Being walked away from, phones going silent, walls going up as you get written off is the most inhumane thing I have ever experienced, and it took me to the depths of despair. It triggered the same total abandonment I experienced as a child and there were many times that I was literally living in hell trying to work out on my own what was happening to me.

This brings me to touch on the subject of menopause in the workplace and the laws in place to protect women during this time. Thankfully, there is legislation in place and menopause is covered under the Equality Act, 2010, that protects three very definite characteristics: age, sex and disability discrimination.

Also, the Health and Safety at Work Act 1974 extends to women when suffering from menopause symptoms and ensuring their working conditions are safe. There are also new codes of practice from ACAS that lay out flexible working conditions for women. Where we are fortunate these days is that employers have to adhere to these policies and guides, but this does not mean we can kick back and trust this will be done. These rules need to be enforced and in order for them to be enforced they need to be known and understood and that is our responsibility to know our rights.

Having been a work addict in the past, I would not take care of myself and would allow my employer to take liberties when it came to my working hours and sick time needed during stressful periods when your hormones can start to make you feel really ill. On top of that, if you are like me and one of your dominant menopause symptoms is insomnia, then going to work the next day can be impossible, so these laws have been passed to protect us.

Talking to your superiors and letting them know what is going on with you and that you are aware of policies that protect you during this time will make things easier for you. Another reason women are unlikely to want to discuss their menopause symptoms is because of the stigma around the subject and also the fact that they themselves do not recognize menopause as a proper illness when in fact it can be considered a disability when it is very severe.

It is a shame that ageing carries with it such a weight for women, and they risk the chance of getting overlooked for promotions and other work opportunities, so we go back to the suffering in silence that only adds more stress to the situation and exacerbates the symptoms even more.

It took me a very long time to understand menopause and the impact it had on my health. Learning how to manage the stress in my life was the most important thing I have done to manage my symptoms. Finally, a few years have passed where I have been able to find the right balance of HRT and after getting rid of toxic people, everything has calmed down. I am no longer ashamed of my story as I feel that the benefits to learning self-care will help me live a much longer, healthier life. The humiliation I experienced for the first years as I allowed so-called experts to play Russian roulette with my hormone medication has subsided and now, I can even find some of it amusing. In all honesty I mainly now just feel grateful to have survived the ordeal and to be in a position to help other women learn about their bodies and help them avoid some of the problems I encountered. I am a better person for the experience and can use my voice to help others. I also have a huge sense of responsibility to share the information I have discovered during this process and feel angry that psychiatry is often the first solution that is sought by other professionals when they come across a woman in menopausal meltdown.

It is a scary thought that for many women, psychiatric drugs were pitched to them by their doctors before Hormone Replacement Therapy (HRT) was even mentioned. I have now been taking HRT since 2015 and without it probably would not be alive to tell the tale. For many women, life without HRT would be unbearable but there are also some dangerous side effects that need to be addressed.

There are two types of HRT: Bioidentical and Synthetic. Bioidentical hormones replicate the molecular structure of your own hormones, oestrogen, progesterone and testosterone. This type of hormone is supposed to function better within your body compared to a synthetic one. Bioidentical hormones are compounded so they can be prescribed in exact dosages that are tailored to your needs. So, accuracy is the main component as to why someone would choose bioidentical over synthetic hormones. Regardless of which you decide is better for you, it is important to find a specialist, not just your regular GP to take you through the process.

Over the years I have really been against having to take any kind of medication and really struggled knowing I was dependent on HRT and on various occasions, on the advice of different experts, I have tried to lower my dosages with a view to coming off it completely. Every single time I had a doctor recommend I change my dosage, there were dramatic consequences as each and every time it triggered insomnia and there I was again, in the emergency room. When you remember that progesterone regulates the blood sugars and hormones assist the brain stem with sleep it is not surprising that my body had a major reaction to any changes especially when they were way too drastic.

One example of getting it seriously wrong was putting a testosterone implant in my body for three months, that almost polished me off. The next big error was when another specialist decided I should change from an oestrogen oral pill to a cream. Bearing in mind I was living in Texas where most days it was one hundred degrees and I was in training for a charity bike ride, it was the worst advice possible because my body did not absorb the cream and when the oestrogen foundation ran out that I had built up over a long period of time, there I was again staring at the ceiling all night. The third time an idiot nurse practitioner cut my oestrogen in half because, after reading my blood work, he decided I was oestrogen dominant. The problem with that was he did way too much too quickly, and it crashed my whole system.

Finally, a few years ago, on returning to England I allowed my GP to yet again change my HRT to what he thought was a better dosage and yet again within a few weeks I noticed I was in major trouble and found out that he had taken my progesterone down from 200mg to 1mg and again it was off to the hospital. I was like a raging diabetic who could not sleep, which is hardly surprising as progesterone is something women produce when they are pregnant as it makes them rest, keeps them calm and helps them sleep.

Finally, I made the decision to stop allowing others to change my prescription. I gave up on the idea to come off HRT and decided it just was not worth the risk to my health any more. For many women, HRT is not something that life is worth living without and I am just one of those women. Since this decision I have not had any issues and feel blessed that my understanding on the subject of menopause has increased to the degree that I can keep myself safe, happy and healthy.

Having had a healthy, few years, I really feel for women who are just hitting the beginning of perimenopause and have no idea what awaits them. The hardest thing to spot for yourself is when the changes start to happen as the symptoms creep up so slowly and are so unnoticeable at first. It is also easy to blame the creeping fatigue down to doing too much, the loss of libido to not being interested in your relationship, sleeplessness is the norm, and you still have not put two and two together.

There are always external factors to use as a justification for feeling like crap or others to blame as to why you feel any of these feelings. The problem in our society is that even our doctors and many of our medical experts and specialists do not fully understand the endocrine system and even when you request a hormone test from your GP, they may be reluctant to allow it as they are not going to be able to read the lab report anyway! On top of this issue, of lack of education in the medical field, we also have the worldwide problem of it being a very expensive process for women in countries such as America where a blood test is hundreds of dollars and then you have to add to that a consultation with an endocrinologist to read the lab report which is even more and that is without even getting a prescription yet. So many women are not in the financial position to afford this and end up putting themselves at the bottom of the list and they start feeling worse each day. It is shocking to think that due to this more and more end up in the psychiatric wards because they have not had the luxury of expert help and assistance at a time in their lives when they need it the most. That is when women become vulnerable and have antidepressants pushed on them as a solution to the symptoms as it is a cheaper option than Hormone Replacement Therapy and all it takes to even be eligible to receive it.

The end of my nightmare came just as quickly as it had begun. On a trip home to England to see my family and spend time with my sister's husband John and his children in Ireland during covid lockdown meant I had to renew my prescription with a British doctor. When I asked him to duplicate what I had been taking in America he was stunned because it turned out that the American dosage of Hormone Replacement Therapy was over four times the legal dosage of what you can prescribe in England. In fact, after further investigation and CT scans, it was discovered I had two massive tumours in my uterus that were the size of large grapefruits. I was told the chances of them being cancer was extremely high due to their size and had to get on the waitlist for surgery which took seven months. The wait was agonizing but I came through a full hysterectomy really well and the best news of all was that the tumours were benign. I am so appreciative of the National Health Service who took such good care of me. There is no doubt the tumours were being fed by the large dose of HRT and contributing to the physical issues I had and since this surgery I am happy to say I have a new lease of life and have not felt this good in many years.

If anyone had told me I would write a book about my worst nightmare and speak publicly about my ordeal and how I survived it I would never have believed it but staying silent will not help others and will not change the laws as to how women are treated in the future. I won't be silent about what happened to me because I know millions of women go through this every single day. So much of how we take care of ourselves depends on how we were raised and what we experienced growing up. The need for people to be heard, validated and acknowledged for their struggles is immense rather than being judged for being human. So many people feel shame and have to remain silent and secretive about their struggles. It is time to share our stories with each other so that we can make the world a better place and change the outcome for others who end up on this path.

Compassion, understanding, education and knowledge is vital in the area of menopause and the endocrine system and the impact it can have on your mind, if we are to protect young women around the world from the same fate of the women who do not make it through.

9

Solutions to Menopause

Menopause has been a hot topic recently. I am happy to say Davina McCall presented a documentary on menopause and whilst it was a great step forward it just scratched the surface. The women who shared their stories were brave, but I felt there was so much not being said that needs to be and hopefully this book has gone a step deeper into what can happen when we neglect ourselves and do not listen to our bodies that are screaming for us to slow down when we suffer endocrine depletion.

I found it interesting that one of the women interviewed had her identity hidden. She was filmed with just a corner of her eye showing as she talked about losing her job due to menopausal symptoms. Here we are talking about empowering women and changing the way women are viewed in menopause and being more open about the issues we face and I found this counter productive to the message. It actually promoted that we should be ashamed of being human beings. The sad fact is that we have not come very far at all if this is as far as we have come. We still cannot show our faces and say "this happened to me" and I survived and am proud of that fact. Only when we can look other women in the eye and tell our story will we truly be empowered. I have been following Penny Lanscaster's menopause journey very closely and thank God that. I loved how supportive her husband Rod Steward was and how he gave us a perspective of what men go through when their loved one is struggling. It is fantastic that someone in the public eye is going further in telling the true reality of what happened to them and not skirting the edges. Thank you Penny for helping so many women and bringing this subject into the open.

Menopause has been called the change and in fact change is what is needed at this time so we can modify our lives to accommodate the stress it is under physically. On the whole change for many people is a super scary thing and can actually create more stress if you cannot embrace it. Good and bad change happens constantly, whether we like it or not, and it is very stressful to try and stop it from happening. Holding something that is not working in place creates a toxic state in the body compared to letting go and accepting change, especially when analytically it is change for the good but habitually, we do not want to let it happen. The need to hold on to a pattern that is not working is very common, especially as you get older. Older and smarter therefore do not always go hand in hand and resisting change for the good can exacerbate fear and anxiety. Change was necessary for me to improve my menopausal symptoms and in all areas of my life including friendships, romantic relationships, career, ideals, beliefs, goals and purposes. Being flexible was such a stretch for me but it was a much better mental state to be in if I could let go of rigid thinking which caused more stress than changing would have done in the first place. So be open to stepping back and looking at your life, at what you have created, at the people you surround yourself with and at the possibility that what you are creating is not necessarily good for you and it may be time to change which will be challenging, but in the long term it will bring you so much more happiness, balance and stability within your endocrine system.

The next concept for me to confront was to find balance and a less stressful way of life during menopause and to educate myself better when it came to my own body, mind and endocrine system. Knowledge is power and understanding how the vicious cycle of stress kept repeating in my life was key to gaining control over it. I figured out the following with my new way of doing mathematics.

Hormonal fluctuations equal stress, physically, emotionally and mentally

Stress plus hormonal changes equals raised cortisol, and lowered serotonin and causes health issues and overwhelm

Menopause and hormonal fluctuations such as oestrogen dominance equals chronic insomnia

Childbirth plus hormonal fluctuations equals stress and sleep deprivation which equals absolute overwhelm and is a major health risk.

The above does not paint a pretty picture for any of us whose lives are less than manageable, but hopefully it serves as a simple example of how connected these issues all are and how they trigger and feed off each other. Making these connections helps me make better decisions and practise better self-care as I can extrapolate the outcome of my choices, decisions and behaviours and catch myself if I am taking on too much. Trust me, I have spent a lifetime thinking I was invincible until menopause literally brought me to my knees and gave me no choice but to put myself first, finally. Menopause turned out to be the best gift of the whole aging process and one that was totally unexpected. I would never want to turn back the clock and have a wrinkle-free face if I had to give up the hard-won knowledge and wisdom I have gained, on my menopause journey.

One of the hardest things to confront and take responsibility for was the fact that I had created so many problems for myself during menopause purely because I did not respect my body and its limitations and how they were changing with age. Looking into the past it is easy to see how not taking care of myself was set up from a very early age. Racing through life and running away from problems was more manageable when I was younger but now the impact that behaviour had on me was just not worth it and change had to happen if I was going to live a long and happy life. One of the hardest lessons I had to learn and the thing I needed to change the most was a simple word in the English language that needed to play a stronger role in my life and that word was NO. I have since discovered it is a full sentence and needs no explanation and is the key to self-care,

The goal is to be able to say NO without any explaining, reasoning, justifying or feelings of discomfort. It was something I needed to get used to because YES had been my favourite word and it had got me into more trouble than anything else.

Here are some examples of the boundaries I set and the things I started saying NO to.

- Victims clawing at my time wanting sympathy and rescuing.
- Toxic work environments no matter how well paid the job is.
- Assholes who are in my vicinity pulling on my time and attention.
- Being a victim and not taking responsibility for situations I create or contribute to.
- People who were out-exchange
- People who were not there for me in troubled times. No matter how many years that friendship went back, if someone is not there for you then that is a deal breaker.

- Compressing time and cramming as much into my day as possible mainly to make others happy.
- Being around passive aggressive people.
- Addictive, obsessive, excessive exercise that was a main contributing factor to my overwhelm. NO riding one hundred and fifty miles per week on my road bike burning myself out.
- Sugar, dairy, alcohol — the worst things you can put in your body during menopause.
- Crazy fad diets that would leave me stressed and starved and mostly did not work.
- Caffeine overuse which ramps up emotions because it is psychoactive and added to the sleep issues.
- No to psychiatric drugs of any kind as they have no solution to the hormone imbalance stress brings about.

If no was to become a word I was comfortable using, then I had to balance it with making a list of the things I would be willing to say yes to. Here are some examples:

- Find hobbies that promote a calm state of mind such as Pilates.
- Eating a balanced, healthy diet of food that promotes good health.
- Learning about nutrition and its natural healing properties.

- Spending time with good friends who are on similar journeys.
- Writing a book as a cathartic experience and to hopefully help women.
- Finding a career that makes me happy.
- Moving home to England to spend more time with my family — something I have missed out on for many years.
- Consistent daily vitamins and minerals in the form of micronutrients that I know heal my mind and body.
- Financial accountability and not spending above my means.
- Being comfortable in the present time and not looking too far back or too far ahead.
- Having good ethics and being a person of honesty and trust.
- Working hard and bringing value to my work environment.
- Creating a successful life.
- Being at peace with my body and not beating myself up any more.
- Respecting stress and the negative impact it can have on my life and those I love.
- Listening to my body on a daily basis and understanding what it is trying to tell me.

All of the above were obviously not going to be done religiously or perfectly. This was just my guide. As I started my self-care journey, I realised I had a huge ridge on it. It was one thing to make all these lists but when I actually started doing them, I felt guilty taking time for myself. I felt horrible saying no to people because sometimes I really wanted to say yes but knew it would tip me over the edge energetically. But I pushed and even turned down job interviews based on my inner sense of knowing if a certain job would bring too much stress into my life.

Maybe I had a preconceived idea that taking time out for myself was selfish that gave me such a problem with self-care. It occurred to me that other women probably have felt the same. Even taking time in the shower or having a bath or putting on make-up and dressing seemed to be things I raced through in life. What if I just slowed everything down by fifty per cent? It was worth a try.

I realised that the way I communicated was also having an effect on my stress levels. I naturally talk quickly, and my mind can work at lightning speed, so slowing that communication process down was tough. How much was I saying that was purely background filler? Almost like thinking aloud and not having an off switch became my normal. In times of stress and overwhelm my sleep patterns would be affected and it seemed that the less I slept the more I talked and the more I noticed everything that was wrong in my environment. It was a compulsion that took over me and it was exhausting for the people around me as they had no idea what was going on or how to shut me up. I notice it may also be a family trait as my mother loves to yap at one hundred miles an hour and her mind jumps all over the place. I realised I was doing exactly the same thing. Not only that but I was also dominating conversations which was awful now I think about it. I had to learn to shut up and listen and not just wait for the other person to finish talking so I could have my turn.

Nutrition is another important factor during menopause. What you put in your body has to contain the healthy ingredients that are going to assist you rather than hinder you and it was one of the first things I looked at when it came to trying to find balance in my life. I knew my eating habits had become worse during menopause and comfort eating became a really bad habit. Even worse was the beating I would give myself afterwards and then of course I would work out like mad to get rid of the calories and it started to trigger a very old eating disorder from years before as I would obsess over each and every calorie but find myself unable to stop raiding the cookie jar. Over time my clothes started to feel tighter and my solution to that was to buy bigger trousers, which was fine except I really hated myself and my lack of control. It felt like I was spiralling down which then made me anxious and depressed with how I looked. It was a vicious circle and so it was time to make some necessary changes if I was to start feeling good about myself and bring the balance I am always talking about back into my life. By this time having been to hell and back during menopause I would have done anything to feel better.

At first, I was very sceptical about how a few vegetables could make any difference, but it turned out they did and the more I added healthier ingredients into my diet the better I felt. Soon I noticed that the days where I ate badly, I also felt like shit and that was no coincidence. The more I looked into it, I realized that basically most of my favourite things are not endocrine system, menopause friendly, including caffeine, alcohol, sugar, meat and dairy. That basically was the total sum of my diet whilst I was living in America and without my noticing, the quantities went up as well.

Some have suggested that Asian women have a much easier time during menopause due to the difference in diet; they consume more vegetables, grains and fish compared to the average Western diet which has a lot more meat which can be full of hormones, steroids and antibiotics that wreak havoc with our already stressed endocrine system. Dairy was also notably less in Asian cuisine, and they did not have the same obesity issues that the Western world is experiencing either so something had to be said for it.

Eating more fruits and vegetables and whole grains is a perfect way to eat during menopause due to their low fat and low-calorie content. A diet high in plant content has a way of balancing out your hormones and minimising side effects such as hot flushes. Caffeine and alcohol are major triggers for this particular symptom. Now I am not saying we all have to go strictly vegan but there are so many benefits to adding this kind of fibre to your diet, including weight loss that it would be hard not to want to at least try.

Soy and soy-based foods are another good menopause food due to the amount of phytoestrogen (dietary oestrogen compounds) they contain which have been known to help with any psychological symptoms in menopause.

The good news is that a plant-based diet is not as bad as it first seems. These days we are fortunate to have so many substitutes for meat and dairy that we can find a way to curb the cravings if we need too. In fact, most supermarket chains now have whole sections dedicated to foods that are free from gluten and toxic ingredients.

There are many foods that contain oestrogen naturally and some of them even taste good such as dark chocolate, tart cherry juice and cruciferous vegetables such as cauliflower, broccoli and Brussel sprouts. These kinds of vegetables are of paramount importance during menopause as they detox the body and stop it building up on bad oestrogen, leaving you with more energy and better sleep.

Just keep in mind for any new regime, a thirty-day programme would be necessary to notice the benefits and after that it's all plain sailing. The good thing to keep in mind is that dark chocolate is full of oestrogen, which is why we tend to crave it at certain times of the month, so knock yourself out, have a few squares a day. It is the one time in life it's good for you to indulge.

I would say these days I am eighty percent plant based instead of twenty per cent and feel so much better for it. I started with a complete detox and did six weeks on a juicing diet by the Juice Master Jason Vale with the idea of just losing a few pounds and getting back on track. What happened after this time was that I did not want to go back to the way I was eating and did not crave or miss any of the bad foods I had given up. Twenty pounds lighter and full of energy, I made the decision to stay plant based most of the time, except for maybe Christmas Day or if I went to a BBQ once in a while. Apart from that there is no way I am giving up how good I feel to eat crap.

Exercise: This brings me to the subject of exercise. You will be surprised to know that less is more as we go through menopause. Those days of pounding the streets running or killing ourselves in the gym is just not going to cut it if you want some calm in your life.

For me, being a workout freak, I hated the way my body was changing during menopause, especially the weight gain around my tummy and the only way I knew how to combat this was to up my exercise which was the worst thing I could do. Funny that it is counter-intuitive to cut down on exercise when you want to lose weight, but that is what you need to do at times so you do not put the body under stress, kick in the cortisol stress hormone and end up tired and comfort eating. .

Now do not get me wrong. I am not saying that regular, sensible exercise is not extremely beneficial. I am really talking to the women who end up doing way too much. During this transition, your body is using a great deal of energy just dealing with the hormonal changes that are happening, and rest and relaxation is really important at this time to be able to stay balanced mentally as well as physically.

Too much exercise can also lead to adrenal fatigue which pushes your body to be running on zero which is never a good thing. I used to think nothing of riding my road bike fifty or sixty miles three or four times a week and as I started to go through menopause, I found that the more I exercised and pumped my body full of endorphins the harder it was to come down and achieve a calm state. The exercise would have to be done in the morning as I would be up all night if it was later than midday which was a disaster considering I was having issues sleeping already.

If you have been hitting it hard at the gym, you may want to switch to more gentle exercises such as simply taking a walk, which has many mental health benefits associated with it as you are more inclined to look out and externalise rather than interiorize and look at your problems if you are walking in nature. Swimming and yoga or Pilates are also great alternatives. Another way to calm down the exercise is to not work out every single day which can be the case as we put on weight and do our best to try and shift it by throwing ourselves full speed into a new workout programme. This is not going to help you as you burn out and just feel even more exhausted. So be gentle with yourself and choose your form of exercise wisely. Give yourselves breaks and rest days and if it helps, try finding a relaxing activity instead of working out now and then.

Compressing Time: Another life-saving decision I made on my way to menopause health was to stop compressing so much into the time I had available to me. For as long as I could remember I had unrealistic expectations on what was achievable in a given segment of time. My to-do list was always so long and although I loved writing them, actually getting them all done, just caused me a massive amount of stress. The same thing was happening when it came to doing things for others and overcommitting myself and making promises that would be exhausting to keep. Letting others down has never been something I was willing to do but it would often turn out that this was exactly what ended up happening as it was just impossible to carry out all that I had committed to. So, I had to take a step back and figure out why I was doing this in the first place and that again went back to my childhood and feeling compelled to finish my chores and be perfect so that there would not be bad consequences. I was driven to get as much as possible done by fear and this became a habit of a lifetime without me even realising it. Compressing time literally means slamming in as much as you can into an amount of time that is too short.

As I went through the process of breaking down this pattern, I also realised that in many situations this had been a one-way street, meaning others had allowed me to do all the running around and not given anything back in return. Fair exchange was not a part of this deal and that was another learned behaviour I would have to break if I were to remain stable and healthy. Pushing back and saying no to people, especially in the workplace was tough at first and came as quite a shock to many. To be honest I was not very graceful about it in the beginning but as time went on, I started to take one day at a time and only planned a couple of things in any day. That way I could always add more if I needed to but most of the time a couple of things were enough.

Sharing your story: I cannot count the number of times my sister and I talked about being a better support system for each other. To be honest we were both so busy getting on with our lives that time went by so fast, and we did not catch up enough. Having a support person and sharing what is going on for you is one of the most valuable things you can do. Choosing the right person to do that with is also vital as you need to know you are going to be heard, without judgement and without that person coming back at you with their own evaluation of what you should do with your issues.

Only we know how to solve our own problems. Of that I am sure, but in order to come to the place of being able to find the right answer, we need to share our story and process the whole picture for ourselves. Having someone tell you what they think you should do is the quickest way to shut someone down and make them feel that they need to keep quiet about their problems. One of the reasons for this is that usually when a person is upset, they will not be viewing the issue from a pan-determined place: it will have a bias for sure. Only after recounting your story a few times, will you be able to see things from a newer, fresher perspective and be able to take someone else's perspective into place. So, choose your person well. It does not even need to be someone you know well; the important part is that you trust them. Make sure you also do the same for them so that you are in fair exchange, and it is not a one-way street. There is nothing worse than dumping all your problems and walking away. For this to work well, both people need time to share and time to listen then it will be successful.

Choosing someone who has been through similar circumstances to you can also be helpful, especially when it comes to menopause and your hormones. I have tried talking to people who have zero understanding of it and it just has not worked for me. I guess it is a bit like someone telling me about their childbirth story; I can listen but would not perhaps relate to the circumstances as well as someone who has shared knowledge and experience on the subject.

Let go of toxic relationships: This one was tough for me but necessary. When I left my last relationship and his family, it was one of the hardest things I have ever done as I loved them all and never believed it would one day end. We were perfect in so many ways but when I got ill and the group got together on their opinions of the situation, it was something that I had to walk away from.

Each and every person in that family was unique, beautiful, special, caring, loving and wonderful but during my hormone issues they would talk to each other about the situation and then the group decision would be formed, and it never came out well for me when that happened. Lost were the good things, the victories we had and the joy we found and memories we made. The focus became very much on the problem. There is a reason a stepmother gets a bad rap and that is partly because they are not her biological children and also because she is the one who is there every day trying to make things go right. Your own mother can fuck up and get away with it and be forgiven far easier than a stepmother ever will, hence we have fairy tales written about how evil we are, and it is all an easy narrative to go along with.

One thing is for sure and that is I walked away knowing I had made this family's life better than I found it. I gave it everything I had to the point of overdoing it. I loved each and every one of those children and there were times when I helped every single person in that family, and they made my life so much better in so many ways regardless of how many problems we had to overcome.

Sometimes to leave because it is the right thing to do for the greatest number of people and for those that you love. These kids had been through enough drama in their lives and the fact I was making it worse was heart-breaking for me. Being able to see their perspective and leave was the most loving thing I could have done for everyone. It has been four years now and being alone has not been easy but at least I have been able to take the time to take care of myself, take responsibility for myself and to turn things around. I would say that is winning.

This list of suggested solutions is just what worked for me, and I hope that some of them can help you too. There is no quick fix through this time of life that is for sure and there is not a one size fits all remedy to get you through the bad days. It is very much a case of trial and error to find out what works. Slowly as you get used to implementing some of the self-care suggestions above you will find it becomes a habit and you will begin to see the difference and be happier with your life and as you are calmer and more aware of your needs your loved ones will sense a difference too.

Gratitude got me a long way as I went through menopause, along with the serenity prayer. Our mind plays tricks on us when we are not feeling great, and we start to only be able to see the bad things in life and focus on what we are not happy with. When you start to be gentle with yourself, the shitty committee in your mind will not like it and may even ramp up for a while but you have the power to control your thoughts and actions and how you treat yourself. Becoming conscious of the part you play in beating yourself up and putting yourself down or just overloading yourself will be the very first big step in stopping the overwhelm.

During my whole journey, the overwhelming thing I am left with is this. I was responsible for my condition, no one else. I was the one driving myself so hard. I was relentless when it came to pushing through days when I was just exhausted and taking on way too much. I was responsible for allowing those closest to me to take advantage and allowed them to constantly create problems for me to solve, in fact I enjoyed being the rescuer and the hero for people as it fed into my self-esteem and made me feel loved and wanted. I now realise this was abusive to myself and had to stop. The saviour complex I had sweeping in and making everything go right for someone else was so dysfunctional because I pretended to have all the solutions for everyone else, but the reality was that I had none for myself.

By focusing on the problems of others I could hide from my own issues and dysfunctions. Menopause gave me the gift of breaking me into a thousand pieces and then I had the choice to decide if I wanted to put myself back together again but a new, improved, better version of myself and that is what I did. Of course, the downside to this new me is that I can upset others by standing my ground and not bending to their wants and needs and not working to their timeline. This is also true of relationships which is why I had not engaged in any for a very long time. I have yet to test this new, improved Annie in that arena, but I have a sneaky feeling it will be fine as I have come so far in knowing who I am and what is right for me.

Writing this book about my most embarrassing, humiliating and shameful moments was not the most fun thing to do at times, but my pride and dignity is not important any more and what others think of me is not important at all. The only thing that really matters is that I have found myself, survived this ordeal, and come out of it stronger and able to really help others in a way that really matters.

As women age, we have to acknowledge it is not an easy journey at all sometimes. It is hard to confront that we are changing in so many ways and are not what we used to be, but we have to acknowledge that we have a unique and special kind of beauty that only comes with surviving these hard-fought battles that leave us bruised and battered but ultimately make us truly know who we are and what we are made of.

Ageing is not a right, it is a privilege that so many like my beloved sister Kay never experience. Let's find a way to embrace this sacred time and honour ourselves and the journey we have been through and support each other.

10

Happy Hormones

I wanted to end this book on a positive note and share the one thing that saved me from history repeating itself. In my search for hormonal stability a word kept popping up that I did not understand, and that word was Cortisol.

By now I had a very good understanding of what the endocrine system was composed of and how it impacted my thoughts, feelings, emotions and most of all my behaviour. It was only when I discovered the importance of Cortisol in the whole subject of hormones that I got my life and health back on track.

Understanding Cortisol, the stress hormone, changed everything for me and I have never looked back. It still amazes me that no one ever mentioned it to me before as it is such an important part of the whole menopause process.

So, Cortisol is a hormone that we all have, and it is produced along with adrenaline from the adrenal glands (that is about as medical as I am going to get about the subject). So, when we experience times of stress or even excitement cortisol is sent through the body as a reactive fight or flight response mechanism. It actually dictates to the body how to act when under threat which is great as it keeps us out of danger but there is one flaw with the system and that is when stress builds up and cortisol is released it can continue to be released into the body if the stress or threat is left unhandled. So just think about women going through the menopause and all the stressful factors they are dealing with on a day-to-day basis. They have teenagers at home, marriage and relationship break ups, financial pressure, health issues, elderly parents and a host of other daily pressures that we just get used to dealing with.

So many times, the cortisol tap is turned on at this time of life and then left on continuously leaving us with a host of unpleasant side effects we simply put down to menopause because they often are the same.

Symptoms of high cortisol are rapid weight gain around the face, chest and stomach, high blood pressure, muscle weakness, mood swings, anxiety, depression, irritability. Low levels of cortisol can cause weakness, fatigue and low blood pressure, dizziness, vomiting and Addison's disease.

So, you can see how easy it is to think all our symptoms are due to menopause and believe there is nothing we can do about it, and we would be wrong in that assumption because chances are for so many the problems are due to stress and high cortisol.

What this means is that we have the ability to improve our condition if we can take out the stress in our lives and this is all I did to get back to feeling good again. It was that simple.

If you think you have high or low cortisol then ask your doctor for a test, you can even order a home urine test to do yourself to see if this is part of the problem. Chances are if you are stressed regularly then your cortisol is high, and you need to make some changes fast in order to feel better.

So now we have this data of how high cortisol can stack up even more physical and mental symptoms on you, what can we do about it? How do we get the cortisol to come down? That is the easy part!

The best way to bring down cortisol is gentle, regular exercise. This helps us to breathe deeply and detox out the excess cortisol. Detoxing out cortisol can also be done with hot Epsom salt lavender baths which works great and helps us sleep. Of course, changing the way you function is important especially if you are allowing stress to make you ill and making the cortisol build up in the first place is key as prevention is so much better than finding a cure. Yes, sorry to say you are responsible for that part. That is where you need to make a list of all the stressful things or people in your life and write down what you are going to do about it. You have to take action and do this step because if you don't then nothing will change. The very first step of this process is to acknowledge that you are responsible for your own health and wellbeing, and you are the only one who can change things for the better.

You have to decide to stop playing the victim, stop blaming others and start to put yourself first, because if you do not then you will create the perfect storm and you could find yourself in a health issue that you cannot come back from. Of course, this is not all just going to happen overnight especially when you have people to deal with who are causing you stress and overwhelm. Trust me, they are not going to like the fact that you have woken up to the truth that they are not a positive factor in your life or that they are completely out of exchange with you and trust me they would prefer things stayed exactly as they are. You may have a struggle on your hands, and you might even have to close the door on certain relationships to create a healthier life for yourself.

One thing I know for sure, is that if I had stayed in my marriage, I would never have gotten healthy and had the time and energy to have worked out what the root of the issue was. There were so many people in my immediate vicinity that were dragging me down and bringing drama and chaos to it that I would never have been able to see what was making me so ill. It really took my sister to point it out for me to come to my senses and have the courage to say, 'enough is enough' and walk away.

We owe it to ourselves to make the right decisions and changes that will be for our benefit long-term. If you are in an unhappy or in an abusive relationship then you cannot hope to feel better whilst you stay in it. So, it is time to look in the mirror and have a heart to heart. Who or what is stressing you out? How is it affecting you mentally, physically and emotionally and what are the steps you need to take to stop the cycle?

Making a plan was the way I got through creating change in my life. I literally wrote down exactly what I needed and wanted in life and started to work my way towards it. I made no sudden moves that would draw anyone's attention to what was going to happen. I just quietly, slowly and without drama just backed away and before anyone realised, I was long gone and once the stress was gone so was the physical roller coaster. I started sleeping better and had time to recover and heal.

The most important change was that I was in charge of my time and in the moment and would notice if I was tired and needed to rest or take a nap and very soon that became the norm for me. Looking back, I had no idea how fast life was speeding up and I am sure my sister had no idea where each day went as she raced through it. It is very fitting that this book was written at my sister's home in Ireland. So many times, I felt her beside me, giving me strength to see the book through and I feel very proud that we have achieved something very special together and hope that it can help you as much as this information helped me. When Kay died, I literally stopped, time stood still, and I cannot remember much for the six months that followed as I was in a fog going from one day to the next barely having the energy to do the basics. Her passing showed me how to slow down to a pace that I needed to deal with the pain and grief of losing not only a beloved sister but a protector and guide through my whole life. It was this tragic event that changed me forever and I just wish I could have learned the lessons without losing her.

I hope you have gained something from my story. I know that I gained a great deal from writing it as it was very cathartic and helped release the frustration and anger of the treatment I received at the hands of doctors and hospitals in my journey through perimenopause and menopause. My hope is that in the future women do not have to suffer in silence and can tell their stories without fear or shame of the stigma that comes with this right-of-passage. As I have mentioned before, aging is not a right, it is a privilege that not all of us get to experience. My goal is to reach as many women as I can with a message of love and understanding for their struggle and journey.

I want to see in my lifetime changes made in the care and education of women about their endocrine system and most of all I want to see the psychiatric abuse of women in menopause come to an end and in its place medical protocols for how women are treated when they have an endocrine crisis. Medical care should be accessible for every woman around the world, not just for those that can afford it.

Women are incredible creatures that bring not only life but nurturing, love, joy, creation and beauty to the world, it is about time we started treating women with the kindness and care they deserve at a time in their lives when they need it the most.

Thank you for taking the time to read my book. Please pass it on to anyone who you think might need this information and the world will be a better and safer place for us all.

We do not have to suffer in silence.